190
READY-TO-USE ACTIVITIES THAT MAKE SCIENCE FUN!

Hooked   ibrary

Published by Jossey-Bass
A Wiley Imprint
989 Market Street, San Francisco, CA 94103-1741 www.josseybass.com

Jossey-Bass books and products are available through most bookstores. To contact Jossey-Bass directly, call our Customer Care Department within the U.S. at (800) 956-7739, outside the U.S. at (317) 572-3993 or fax (317) 572-4002.

Jossey-Bass also publishes its books in a variety of electronic formats. Some content that appears in print may not be available in electronic books.

ISBN 0-7879-6601-0

Printed in the United States of America
FIRST EDITION
PB Printing
10 9 8 7 6 5 4 3

GEORGE WATSON

Acknowledgments and thanks for your professional support in writing the "Hooked on Learning" series. I've truly "hooked" up with the best crew.

MARLENE TILFORD
Advisor

JON GILLIES
Advisor

ESTHER JOHNSON
Jiffy Steno Services

ALAN ANTHONY
Illustrator

ACKNOWLEDGMENTS

Karen Auchstaetter
John Hall
Mary Johnston
Walter Kostyna

Mel Kozlowski
Kim LaFreniere
Carolyn Monette
Les Richardson

Patty Serwotki
Fred Sykes
Jack Umstatter

ABOUT THE AUTHOR

George Watson (B.A., University of Saskatchewan, Saskatoon, Saskatchewan, Canada) taught almost every subject including major academic subjects, special education, physical education, and art at the elementary and junior high levels during his teaching career. Mr. Watson recently retired after 28 years of service in the classroom and now dedicates his time to writing and to the building of a 1934 Ford street rod.

Mr. Watson is the author of *The Classroom Discipline Problem Solver, Teacher Smart: 125 Tested Techniques for Classroom Management and Control, 190 Ready-to-Use Activities that Make English Fun!*, and *190 Ready-to-Use Activities that Make Math Fun!* (published by Jossey-Bass, an imprint of John Wiley & Sons).

Mr. Watson also conducts in-service programs for teachers, parent–teacher associations, and health organizations. Mr. Watson has also authored several short stories for magazines and a book on street rodding skills. He can be contacted at **geobravo396@hotmail.com**.

ABOUT THE HOOKED ON LEARNING LIBRARY

The *Hooked on Learning Library* is a comprehensive, three-book series featuring teacher- and student-friendly activity sheets for the secondary classroom in the areas of English, Mathematics, and Science.

In writing these books, special effort was taken to understand students from a social, emotional, and cultural perspective. The result of that initiative is that the books are filled with highly-charged, attention-grabbing, and relevant activity sheets that not only cover the content, but also are fun to do.

An excellent educational resource, this series can be used to provide immediate skill reinforcement and to address skill attainment problems, or it can be used as an integral part of the long-term planning of English, Mathematics, and Science programs. *Hooked on Learning* not only fulfills the needs of the "at-risk" student, but it also satisfies the needs of the strong, independent, self-reliant learner.

The three books in the *Hooked on Learning Library* are:

- 190 Ready-to-Use Activities that Make English Fun!
- 190 Ready-to-Use Activities that Make Math Fun!
- 190 Ready-to-Use Activities that Make Science Fun!

All three books in the *Hooked on Learning Library* have unique areas called Quick Access Information pages. These pages target important information and skills to be learned or reinforced. The Quick Access Information data in this science book is presented in the form of compact or concise completion paragraphs that summarize key points or strategic data that relate to the particular section.

ABOUT THIS BOOK

This science volume was a joy to write. Every effort was made to continue the basic theme of the "Hooked on Learning" series, that is, to make learning fun. In addition, each page was designed to grab and hold students' attention. Thus, problem solving, brainstorming, challengers, word associations, scramblers, "double deckers," tripod connections, and reverse questions are only a few of the activities used to motivate students and encourage critical thinking.

Although rapid advances continue to occur in many scientific fields, this science edition targets those aspects of the core science curriculum that are not subject to a great deal of change. This approach prevents *190 Ready-to-Use Activities that Make Science Fun!* from becoming dated quickly and makes it useful to educators for years to come.

All 190 activities in this volume enrich and reinforce day-to-day instruction in the fundamental concepts of science. Those concepts are in the areas of the scientific method, earth science, the solar system and the universe, chemistry, physical science, life science, water and erosion, and weather and climate.

Like all books in the "Hooked on Learning" series, this science edition will be a wonderful asset when a substitute teacher is needed in the classroom. The self-contained, high-interest curriculum-based activity pages give the teacher prepared, instant resources she or he will feel totally comfortable using even when the substitute is not familiar with the subject area.

Throughout this book, as in all the books in the "Hooked on Learning" series, you will see strategically placed "Quick Access Information" flags. These flags point out pages that contain concise information puzzles. These puzzles, or completion paragraphs, focus on and summarize the key points related to the science topic, thus enhancing learning.

190 Ready-to-Use Activities that Make Science Fun! is an effective tool for students of all ability levels. There is something here for everyone—from the at-risk student to the independent high achiever. Here are descriptions of the sections you'll find in this book:

- **Section 1, Laying the Groundwork for Earth Science,** leads the way by presenting fundamental aspects or areas of Geoscience/Earth Science in a unique, stimulating way. The "Earth Science Vocabulary Vowelless Puzzle" is a wonderful example of this. Students are not only challenged to learn the vocabulary, but they have the added concept of replacing vowels in the answer as they go along.

- **Section 2, Essential Strategies for the Scientific Method,** presents high-interest and motivating ideas that relate to the vast area of study involving the scientific method. You'll find activities on the early understandings of the hypothesis concept. For example, "Francis Bacon: Hypothesis and Scientific Inquiry" looks at how Bacon's intellect led to the acceptance of the hypothesis idea as an integral part of modern scientific inquiry.

- **Section 3, Revolving and Rotating with the Solar System,** looks at those core curriculum concepts that relate to the solar system in which we exist and study. "One Famous Astronaut Writes to Another" is a favorite of mine, whereby students are called upon to do creative science writing. They are asked to finish a letter from one famous astronaut (John Glenn) to another famous astronaut (Neil Armstrong).

- **Section 4, Universe Concepts, Puzzles, and Ideas to Stimulate and Enrich,** presents areas of universe and space study that help students stay on task and really enjoy this area of science. A good example is "Universe Study Reverse Questions," for which students are called upon to change their paradigm and make the question suit the given answer. This reinforces learning because of the unique approach to the needed data.

- **Section 5, Chemistry: Fundamental Skill Builders,** looks at the basic introductory ideas in chemistry study. "Chemistry Vocabulary" is a good example of a high-interest, mind-stretching activity that will grab the students' attention. Students are asked to search a puzzle grid for chemistry words that are related to particular areas.

- **Section 6, Physical Science Concepts for the Modern Classroom,** presents ideas in a motivating way. "Friction Grids," for example, teaches information about friction in a highly interesting puzzle format. It nails down almost all the relevant introductory information students need on this physical science topic.

- **Section 7, Hooked on Life Science Techniques, Ideas, and Concepts,** presents students with different approaches to the enjoyment of life science. "Speedy Cell Knowledge Reinforcement Puzzles" is a great example. It gives students three interesting and unique puzzle forms to work on that enrich the learning of basic life science expressions.

- **Section 8, Water and Erosion Facts and Insights,** looks at how water and related erosion activities have affected the Earth. Again, all the puzzles and high-interest pages are developed to maintain and keep students' interest. "A Two-Space Water Puzzle" asks students to place two answers in each sentence, thereby doubling the data needed. In the process, it makes students think because more of the sentence information is missing, making it more difficult to answer quickly and randomly.

- **Section 9, Understanding the Processes and Cycles of Weather and Climate,** targets fundamental knowledge of how and why the weather and climate processes function. "What Is It? Knowing Weather Patterns from Descriptions" is a great example because students need to read and develop an understanding of the data presented in order to come up with the correct answer.

Throughout this book you will see that I developed strong use of high-interest formats while targeting the core of the curriculum. These high-interest worksheets are necessary in today's classroom where many students need learning processes to grab and maintain their concentration in order to complete tasks. Indeed, the on-task classroom is a happier place for all concerned—not only in the short term but for the long-term learning of the necessary curriculum-based information.

All in all, I know you will enjoy using this science book in the Hooked on Learning series. It will be a totally unique, fresh, and worthwhile addition to the on-going dynamics of your classroom. Like the two other books in this series, it was a joy to write and I know it will be a joy to use.

George Watson

CONTENTS

SECTION 2
ESSENTIAL STRATEGIES FOR THE SCIENTIFIC METHOD   31

SECTION 3
REVOLVING AND ROTATING WITH THE SOLAR SYSTEM   55

SECTION 4
UNIVERSE CONCEPTS, PUZZLES, AND IDEAS
TO STIMULATE AND ENRICH   75

SECTION 5
CHEMISTRY: FUNDAMENTAL SKILL BUILDERS 91

SECTION 6
PHYSICAL SCIENCE CONCEPTS
FOR THE MODERN CLASSROOM 103

SECTION 7
HOOKED ON LIFE SCIENCE TECHNIQUES, IDEAS, AND CONCEPTS   137

SECTION 8
WATER AND EROSION FACTS AND INSIGHTS   173

SECTION 9
UNDERSTANDING THE PROCESSES AND CYCLES OF WEATHER AND CLIMATE   189

SECTION 1

LAYING THE GROUNDWORK FOR EARTH SCIENCE

1. The Earth: A Real Puzzler

★ Study the Choice Box. Find the word that should appear in each numbered blank located in the paragraphs. Write the correct word for the numbered blank on the left. No word may be used more than once.

QUICK ACCESS
information

1. _____

2. _____

3. _____

4. _____

5. _____

6. _____

7. _____

8. _____

9. _____

10. _____

11. _____

12. _____

13. _____

14. _____

15. _____

16. _____

17. _____

18. _____

19. _____

20. _____

People study the 1 for a variety of reasons. Chief among these is the fact that the Earth and its 2 are becoming more closely related to our 3 lives. Since the book *Silent Spring* by Rachel 4 , people have become more aware of our need to care for and 5 the physical 6 . The Earth is directly affected by environmental 7 . The old adage "You 8 what you 9 " alarmingly applies to the Earth and its environment.

An unaware bulldozer operator in the ecologically 10 northern 11 , for example, spelled out the word "HI" with the treads of his machine many years ago. The word is still there and becoming more and more of an ecological 12 to the environment of the 13 landscape as 14 goes on.

We must study the Earth to know the 15 interactions 16 the various Earth processes as we search out the natural 17 of our planet. We are part of the Earth's physical, 18 , and social climate and the 19 we know, the 20 our life will be in, upon, and with it.

CHOICE BOX

scar	processes	between	environment	Northern
better	reap	pollution	daily	Earth
Carson	permafrost	sensitive	time	nurture
ecological	more	resources	complex	sow

2. Earth Science Vocabulary

★ Below are two lists of earth science vocabulary words or phrases. Match the word on the left with the word or phrase on the right that is *related* to it by placing the appropriate number in the space provided. Then locate the word on the left in the left-side puzzle, and locate and circle its related word or phrase in the right-side puzzle. The first one is done for you.

10 crust		1. atomic particle
_____ igneous		2. wind
_____ asteroid		3. dew
_____ equinox		4. cyclone
_____ atom		5. sedimentary
_____ hydrosphere		6. moon
_____ convection		7. water
_____ condensation		8. solstice
_____ hurricane		9. meteor
_____ eclipse		10. core

Left Side

O	A	R	O	O	E	T	E	O	P	R	I	H	M	E
C	O	N	D	E	N	S	A	T	I	O	N	Y	D	Q
B	R	W	O	P	C	R	P	A	G	H	E	D	T	U
W	E	J	U	N	C	R	U	S	T	W	C	R	U	I
A	T	O	M	U	P	W	T	T	J	T	L	O	P	N
H	U	R	R	I	C	A	N	E	T	R	I	S	I	O
I	G	N	E	O	U	S	U	R	B	A	P	P	O	X
I	V	Y	W	P	Q	U	K	O	P	L	S	H	W	G
M	C	O	N	V	E	C	T	I	O	N	E	E	V	H
C	R	U	O	P	W	R	E	D	H	M	T	R	O	O
R	O	M	W	E	T	C	X	Y	L	Y	I	E	W	J

Right Side

S	O	L	S	T	I	C	E	T	V	W	O	U	T	S
A	T	O	M	I	C	P	A	R	T	I	C	L	E	E
U	E	T	P	R	Y	T	R	E	R	N	E	R	V	D
N	I	W	Y	T	C	Q	U	I	S	D	R	A	T	I
I	U	A	O	P	L	P	T	A	V	E	T	U	E	M
V	R	T	G	M	O	O	N	O	M	W	S	T	U	E
W	A	E	H	J	N	V	A	P	E	R	T	G	S	N
X	L	R	U	B	E	R	U	S	T	R	I	P	A	T
P	K	B	U	L	M	T	R	U	W	E	V	G	H	A
W	P	V	J	K	E	W	B	O	M	E	T	E	O	R
C	O	R	E	B	R	E	K	T	F	A	S	Y	T	Y

3. Mineral Identification

★ Read the sentences below. They each describe "in other words" some characteristic of minerals. Your task is to pick the correct word from the Choice Box that would replace the underlined words in the sentence.

1. A major property of minerals is their <u>analysis of their reflection of their specific part of the spectrum</u>. _____

2. We can identify a mineral by the way light reflects from its surface. This is called <u>the bright and flashy reflection</u>. _____

3. <u>The feeling of gravitational exertion</u> can tell us how heavy a mineral feels.

   _____

4. When we rub a mineral against a rough white surface, it shows the property of a <u>long mark on a school chalkboard or a fast drawn line</u>. _____

5. The mineral property of <u>the extent of surface roughness</u> can be discovered by running your fingers over the surface of the mineral. _____

6. The <u>rough, jagged edge or erratic line pattern of the separation</u> of parts of a mineral will help indicate or identify it. _____

7. The <u>smooth, non-jagged edge or clean and exact line pattern of separation</u> of a mineral will help indicate or identify it. _____

8. A mineral's <u>strong opposition to force</u> is its resistance to being scratched.

   _____

CHOICE BOX

luster	streak	cleavage	texture
color	hardness	heft	fracture

4. Geoscience Word Completions

★   Listed below are two sets of 16 Geoscience-related words. Use all 26 letters of the alphabet *only once per set* to complete the words below.

SET A

A	B	C	D	E	F	G	H	I	J	K	L	M	N	O	P	Q	R	S	T	U	V	W	X	Y	Z

1. RI__T __ONE
2. A __ IS
3. TOPOGRAP___
4. __AL__EY
5. __LACIER
6. STAC__
7. __TALAC__ITE
8. __UARRY

9. STAL__G__ITE
10. STRI__MI__E
11. SU__ __UCTION
12. E__OS__ON
13. PLAT__ TECT__NI__S
14. L__STER
15. __ATER TABLE
16. __OINT

SET B

A	B	C	D	E	F	G	H	I	J	K	L	M	N	O	P	Q	R	S	T	U	V	W	X	Y	Z

1. L__NDSLIDE
2. __ET __TREAM
3. __RE
4. MI__ERA__
5. MO__O
6. MA__MA
7. __IND
8. __AR__ON

9. LI__HOS__HE__E
10. LA__A
11. IN__E__ __OSSIL
12. __ __ART__
13. G__ODE
14. __ETTLE LAKE
15. __GNEOUS
16. SEDI__ENTAR__

5. Volcanic "Same As" Vocabulary

★ Many things in Earth Science have similarities, even though at first they may appear to be very different. Your task is to describe how the first item (A) is somehow like the second item (B). Be sure to use complete, proper sentences for your answers.

1. (A)   Magma   (B)   Lava

_____

_____

2. (A)   Block lava   (B)   Aa lava

_____

_____

3. (A)   Volcanic dust   (B)   Volcanic cinders

_____

_____

4. (A)   Volcanic bombs   (B)   War bombs

_____

_____

5. (A)   Shield volcano   (B)   Composite volcano

_____

_____

6. (A)   Volcano   (B)   Earthquake

_____

_____

7. (A)   Tsunami   (B)   Normal ocean wave

_____

_____

6. Volcano Expressions with Missing Letters

★ The words below have every second pair of letters missing. Read the clue, then choose the correct missing pairs of letters for each word from the Choice Box. Each pair will be used once.

CLUES

1. Magma at the Earth's surface

   | LA | |

2. Smooth or rounded surface lava

   | PA | | EH | |

3. Where magma comes out

   | | RF | | E |

4. Mountain building area of volcanoes

   | | NT | | EN | | L |

5. Tida waves

   | TS | | AM | |

6. Rapid lava flow

   | ER | | TI | |

7. Occurs in volcano areas

   | | RT | | UA | | S |

8. Volcano created by violent eruptions

   | CO | | OS | | E |

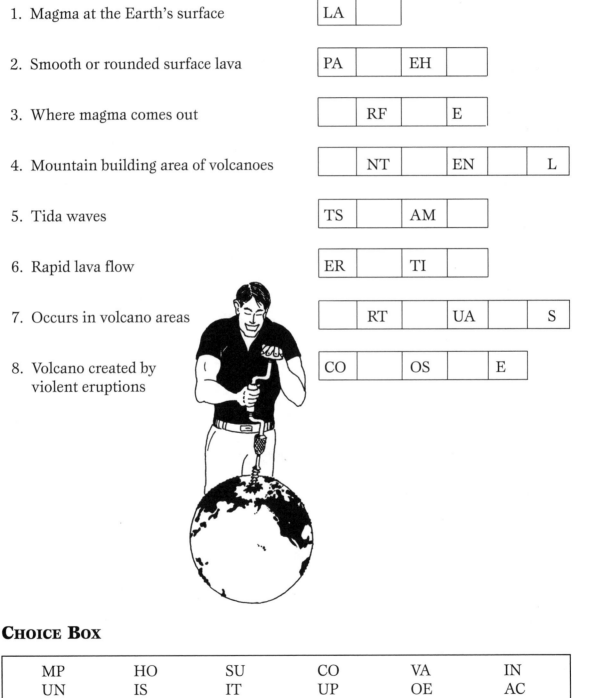

CHOICE BOX

MP	HO	SU	CO	VA	IN
UN	IS	IT	UP	OE	AC
TA	ON	EA	HQ	KE	

NAME _____ DATE _____

7. Researching Famous Geoscientists

★ The following is a list of famous geoscientists. Your task is to look for these people in the encyclopedia and describe their major accomplishments in as much detail as possible using the headings given. You may use another sheet of paper, if necessary.

Alfred Wegener   (Born _____; Died _____)

Area of Work/Study: _____

Two Life Facts or Contributions: _____

_____

_____

Isaac Newton   (Born _____; Died _____)

Area of Work/Study: _____

Two Life Facts or Contributions: _____

_____

_____

James Hutton   (Born _____; Died _____)

Area of Work/Study: _____

Two Life Facts or Contributions: _____

_____

_____

Johannes Kepler   (Born _____; Died _____)

Area of Work/Study: _____

Two Life Facts or Contributions: _____

_____

_____

8. Earth Science Vocabulary Vowelless Puzzle

★ Listed in the Choice Box are some of the most important words associated with Earth Science. Your task is to find and circle the correct Earth Science words in the puzzle. All of the vowels (A, E, I, O, U, Y) have been removed. Write the vowels in place as you find the words.

CHOICE BOX

IGNEOUS	CRATER	DIKE	LAVA	OASIS
ABRADE	ALLUVIAL	FOSSIL	GEOTHERMAL	MAGMA
SEDIMENTARY	BERM	EPICENTER	MANTLE	BUTTE
AVALANCHE	ERUPT	EROSION	MINERAL	METAMORPHIC

9. Volcanoes: Eliminating the Negative and Explaining "Why"

★ This assignment is unusual because you are *not* to choose the correct answer to fit into the space in each sentence. Instead, *you must choose (circle) the least correct answer*. There are three possible answers at the end of each sentence. One is absolutely correct or true, one could be true, and one is false or completely wrong. You must explain *why* the answer you circled is completely wrong or incorrect, or how it does not fit the context of the sentence.

1. A ____ is an instrument that detects earthquake waves.

   seismograph   **Richter Scale**   **telegraph**

   _____

   _____

2. The center part of the Earth is the ____.

   core   **middle**   **crust**

   _____

   _____

3. ____ is the name of molten rock below the Earth's surface.

   Lava   **Delta**   **Magma**

   _____

   _____

4. Giant ocean waves called ____ are caused by earthquakes.

   tidal waves   **tsunamis**   **waves of the Eclipse**

   _____

   _____

5. Large fragments about a meter in diameter flung out of volcanoes are called ____.

   cinders   **bombs**   **hypothesis**

   _____

   _____

10. Fast Changes to the Earth's Surface

★ Match the cause of each fast change to the Earth's surface with its effect by writing the number on the line. Most effects are used more than once.

CAUSE

1. Tornado

2. Hurricane

3. Flood

4. Avalanche

5. Drought

6. Volcano

7. Forest fire

8. Earthquake

EFFECT

_1, 2, 3, 5, 7,_ destruction of forest, loss of animal life

_1, 2, 3, 5,_ loss of crops and income

_8, 1, 2, 3, 4, 6, 7,_ displacement of people, loss of homes

_1, 2, 3, 4, 6, 7,_ massive destruction; possible loss of life

_3, 4, 6,_ burial of skiers, hikers, and so on

_2, 3, 6, 5, 7,_ cracking of soil surface

_1, 4, 7, 8_ upheavals of land forms

_3, 7,_ disruption of such services as electricity

_2, 3,_ possible contamination of ground water

_2, 3, 7,_ refreshing the landscape for new growth

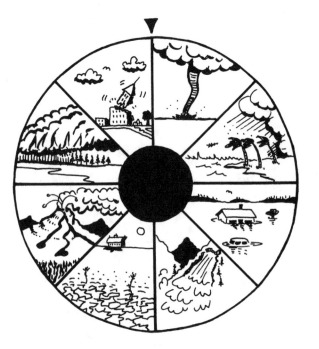

11. Geoscience "Not the Same As" Vocabulary: Part One

★ Read each sentence starter below. Each one states that a particular Earth Science term is not the same as another. Your task is to explain how they are different.

1. Lava is not the same as magma because _____

    _____

2. Soil is not the same as mineral because _____

    _____

3. Water table is not the same as aquifer because _____

    _____

4. Topography is not the same as geology because _____

    _____

5. Tributary is not the same as meander because _____

    _____

6. Stalactite is not the same as stalagmite because _____

    _____

7. Gem is not the same as talc because _____

    _____

8. Strata is not the same as bedrock because _____

    _____

9. Saturation is not the same as segregation because _____

    _____

10. Sedimentary rock is not the same as igneous rock because _____

    _____

12. Geoscience "Not the Same As" Vocabulary: Part Two

★   Read each sentence starter below. Each one states that a particular Earth Science term is not the same as another. Your task is to explain how they are different.

1. Moraine is not the same as talus because _____
   _____

2. Oasis is not the same as desert because _____
   _____

3. Fiord is not the same as bay because _____
   _____

4. Inertia is not the same as energy because _____
   _____

5. Erupt is not the same as erode because _____
   _____

6. Luster is not the same as streak because _____
   _____

7. Ore is not the same as mineral because _____
   _____

8. Geyser is not the same as spring because _____
   _____

9. Lagoon is not the same as river because _____
   _____

10. Latitude is not the same as longitude because _____
    _____

13. Finding Continental Drift Words and Names from Clues and Scrambles

★ The descriptions in Column 1 are clues to finding the word or name you need for Column 2. Column 2 is the word you need for Column 3; however, it is scrambled. Place the unscrambled word in Column 3.

Column 1—Clues	Column 2	Column 3
1. The Earth's top layer	SURTC	_ _ _ _ _
2. Was first to say continents drifted	EERNEGW	_ _ _ _ _ _ _
3. Made theory popular in the 1960s	LONSIW	_ _ _ _ _ _
4. What the sea floor is doing	GRAISPEDN	_ _ _ _ _ _ _ _ _
5. The other name for "continental drift"	AELPT STTECOCIN	_ _ _ _ _ _ _ _ _ _ _ _
6. Amount of continental movement per year	M2C	_ _ _
7. The Earth's second layer	ATENML	_ _ _ _ _ _
8. Clue 3's theory developed due to this continental feature	APSHE	_ _ _ _ _
9. Force associated with tectonics	AKQTAEHREU	_ _ _ _ _ _ _ _ _ _
10. Developed an earthquake scale	CHRTRIE	_ _ _ _ _ _ _
11. Earthquake start point in crust	CSUOF	_ _ _ _ _
12. Continental mark boundaries are these	SKARCC	_ _ _ _ _ _
13. Giant ocean wave	UNIMTSA	_ _ _ _ _ _ _
14. Particles thrown out of volcanoes	SMOBB	_ _ _ _ _

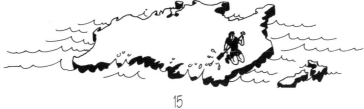

14. How One Thing Is Like Another in Rock Study

★ Many things in rock study have similarities even though at first they may appear to be very different. Your task is to describe in a complete, proper sentence how the first item (A) is somehow like the second item (B). Use the back of this sheet for your answers.

1. (A) Igneous Rock (B) Metamorphic Rock

2. (A) Heat (B) Pressure

3. (A) Basaltic Magma (B) Granite Magma

4. (A) Foliated Rocks (B) Non-foliated Rocks

5. (A) Intrusive Rocks (B) Extrusive Rocks

6. (A) Rock Cycle (B) Change

7. (A) Texture (B) Composition

8. (A) Volcano (B) Fault

15. Geoscience Tripod Connections

★ Listed below are 14 sets of three words that all have something in common in the study of geoscience. Identify what they have in common and write your answer in the space provided. A dictionary or glossary will help.

1.	strata	Carbon 14	epoch	?
2.	mineral	stalagmite	stalactite	?
3.	geyser	water table	geothermal action	?
4.	magma	lava	molten	Volcano
5.	Triassic	Jurassic	Mississippian	?
6.	tsunami	wave	tide	Water (strong)
7.	metamorphic	igneous	sedimentary	Rock
8.	axis	apogee	perigee	?
9.	core	crust	mantle	Earth
10.	monsoon	jet stream	doldrums	Water
11.	dune	desert	silicon	Sand
12.	cyclone	tornado	hurricane	Wind
13.	fossil	amber	coal	Fossil Fuel
14.	porous	permeability	aquifer	?

WE HAD A GEM OF A DAY.

WE HAD A HARD DAY.

16. Geoscience Newspaper Headlines

★ Here are two unusual newspaper headlines. Each one describes some sort of unusual situation. Your task is to write the rest of the newspaper story in the space provided. Include as many scientific details as possible. (You may continue on another sheet of paper, if necessary.) A Choice Box of science-related words is provided.

GLACIER ADVANCING RAPIDLY FROM THE NORTH—DISASTER IMMINENT

_____

_____

_____

_____

_____

_____

"OLD FAITHFUL" GEYSER STOPS—BRILLIANT STUDENT HELP SOUGHT TO RESTORE

_____

_____

_____

_____

_____

_____

CHOICE BOX

aquifer, energy, alluvial, artesian, buoyancy, cirque, decomposition, pressure, force, stress, ore, mineral, esker, flood, geothermal, current, mudflow, outwash plain, precipitation, placer, piedmont

NAME _____   DATE _____

17. Science Problem-Solving with Brainstorming

★   Your class will get into groups of not more than 5 members each. Each student is to use this sheet. You are to discuss the central problem and come up with the most workable solution. Here are the brainstorming rules:

- There are no wrong responses.
- No one is allowed to criticize someone else's response.
- Try to arrive at the most workable answer to the problem.
- Use responses from yourself and others to get better solutions.
- There are 12 possible responses to help solve the problem. Write them below.

Problem: **How to stop the authorities from building a hospital near the San Andreas Fault.**

1. _____
2. _____
3. _____
4. _____
5. _____
6. _____
7. _____
8. _____
9. _____
10. _____
11. _____
12. _____

Most workable solution: _____

Problem: **How to protect your coastline from tsunamis.**

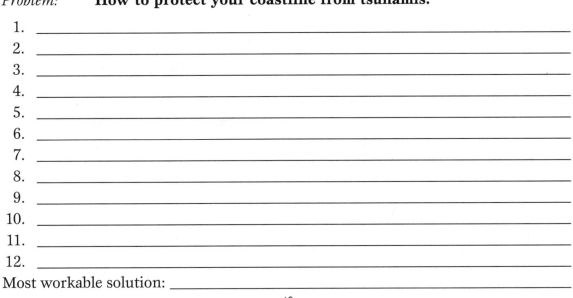

1. _____
2. _____
3. _____
4. _____
5. _____
6. _____
7. _____
8. _____
9. _____
10. _____
11. _____
12. _____

Most workable solution: _____

18. Fossils: Part One

★ Pick the word from the Choice Box to complete the paragraphs. Write your answers on the numbered blanks on the left.

1. _____

2. _____

3. _____

4. _____

5. _____

6. _____

7. _____

8. _____

9. _____

10. _____

11. _____

12. _____

13. _____

14. _____

15. _____

16. _____

17. _____

18. _____

19. _____

20. _____

In order to _1_ as a fossil, an object must be _2_, naturally _3_, and show evidence to prove that an organism _4_ in the past. A wing impression or a _5_ can be a fossil because each is _6_ of pre-existing life.

Many fossils have been _7_. In Siberia, some hunters found a frozen wooly _8_. It was so well frozen that the hunters thought they had found a meat mine. Some fossils are preserved in the _9_ from ancient _10_. This sap _11_ insects, then over time, it turned into a rock-hard substance called _12_.

Many ice-age animals were captured by _13_. Their bodies are usually well preserved because the decay process was _14_ down.

If the conditions were right, only the hard parts of animal bodies survived as fossil evidence. These parts were the _15_, bones, and _16_. In other cases, _17_ ash or ooze on the sea floor covered an animal, thereby preserving it as a fossil.

In the process of becoming _18_, body or wood parts are replaced by minerals, creating a replica of the organism in hardened mineral-rich stone. By the same process, often a _19_ of a shell is formed on the sea floor because the shell _20_ away slowly, leaving only an impression of the organism.

HERE'S ONE FOR THE GEOSCIENTISTS.

CHOICE BOX

slowed	volcanic	mammoth	prehistoric	qualify
evidence	trees	shells	frozen	sap
amber	teeth	dissolved	captured	preserved
footprints	existed	tar pits	petrified	mold

19. Fossils: Part Two

QUICK ACCESS
information

★ Pick the word from the Choice Box to complete the paragraphs.
Write your answers on the numbered blanks on the left.

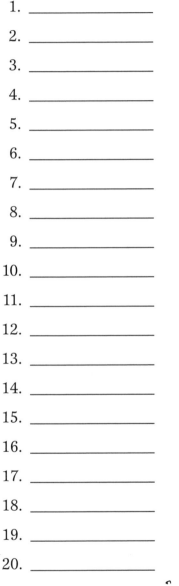

1. _____

2. _____

3. _____

4. _____

5. _____

6. _____

7. _____

8. _____

9. _____

10. _____

11. _____

12. _____

13. _____

14. _____

15. _____

16. _____

17. _____

18. _____

19. _____

20. _____

Because a fossil is a __1__ of past life that is __2__ in or on the earth, it does not necessarily need to be the actual __3__ of the organism. It can take the form of __4__ proof, such as a __5__ fossil. Ancient herd __6__ are examples of trace fossils.

When we __7__ fossils, they give us __8__ to the environment at the time the organism existed. Certain organisms such as ferns and some types of animals could only exist in a very __9__ climate. If evidence of __10__ plants are found in Arctic or Antarctic __11__ (permanently frozen ground), we know the __12__ was much warmer in that __13__ in ancient times. If a fossil or clam shell is found near the top of an __14__ area, such as a hill or __15__, we can deduce that the area was at one time under __16__.

When we look at the layering of rock, it __17__ tells us that the fossils in the __18__ layer of material are older than the layers above it. When scientists study fossil evidence, they can see that many forms of life __19__ longer exist. Studying fossils is fascinating and ongoing because less than __20__ of fossils and ancient life evidence has been found.

> I CAN'T FIND THE FOSSIL ANYWHERE.

CHOICE BOX

logically	preserved	trace	permafrost	clues
body	mountain	record	water	no
warm	footprints	2 %	find	elevated
location	ancient	supportive	climate	bottom

21

20. Geoscience Search from Clues

★ The partially spelled geoscience words, phrases, and terms below are related to or defined by the information or clue under each one. Your task is to complete the word, phrase, or term using the data or clues. A Choice Box has been provided.

1. L __ __ __
   (*magma*)

2. V __ __ C __ __ __
   (*mountain*)

3. __ __ ERM __ __
   (*heat*)

4. __ __ TA __ __ __ PH __ __
   (*rock type*)

5. __ __ C __ C __ CL __
   (*rock change process*)

6. L __ __ G __ CR __ __ __ __ __ __
   (*result of slow rock cooling*)

7. Q __ __ __ __ __
   (*silicon and oxygen*)

8. IG __ __ __ __ __
   (*rock type*)

9. P __ __ S __ __ __ __
   (*force*)

10. A __ __ AD __
    (*to wear away*)

11. __ __ __ D
    (*dry climate*)

12. __ UO __ AN __ __ __
    (*upward force*)

13. __ LE __ V __ __ E
    (*to split along planes*)

14. CO __ __ __ I __ __
    (*to bond together*)

15. ER __ P __
    (*to burst forth*)

16. __ R __
    (*part of geologic time*)

17. __ __ __ S __ __ __ __
    (*movement of surface particles*)

18. __ STU __ __ __
    (*where river current meets tide*)

19. F __ __ __ T __ __ __
    (*uneven breaking in a mineral*)

20. __ __ __ __ Z __ __ __ __ __ __ __ T
    (*temperature when liquid becomes solid*)

21. EX __ __ __ __ AT __ __ __
    (*peeling rock surface layers*)

22. F __ __ D
    (*a bend in the strata of rock*)

23. __ EI __ M __ __ __ __ __ H
    (*measures Earth vibration*)

24. S __ LU __ __ __
    (*capable of being dissolved*)

25. T __ __ __ __ __ __ PH __
    (*surface features*)

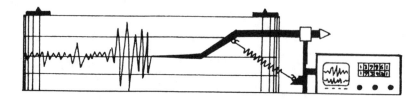

CHOICE BOX

LARGE CRYSTALS	QUARTZ	LAVA	METAMORPHIC	SOLUBLE
EXFOLIATION	IGNEOUS	ARID	ABRADE	EROSION
ERUPT	PRESSURE	ERA	SEISMOGRAPH	VOLCANO
THERMAL	BUOYANCY	COHESION	FREEZING POINT	ROCK CYCLE
CLEAVAGE	FOLD	ESTUARY	FRACTURE	TOPOGRAPHY

21. Earthquake and the Earth's Interior Adjectives

In our study of earthquakes and the Earth's interior, we look at many things, processes, and systems that can be better understood if we can describe aspects of each one.

★   Use <u>adjectives</u> to describe the following *things* associated with earthquakes and the Earth's interior.

(1) Faults	(2) Seismograph	(3) Richter Scale
(4) Tsunami	(5) Epicenter	(6) Moho

★   Use <u>adjectives</u> to describe the following *processes* and *systems* associated with earthquakes and the Earth's interior.

(1) Compression	(2) Buoyancy	(3) Isostasy
(4) Elastic Energy	(5) Tension	(6) Continental Drift

22. Geoscience Adjectives

In our study of Earth Science, we look at many things, processes, and systems that can be better understood if we can describe aspects of each one.

★ Use <u>adjectives</u> to describe the following Geoscience *things*.

(1) Bedrock	(2) Magma	(3) Igneous Rocks
(4) Sedimentary Rocks	(5) Metamorphic Rocks	(6) Minerals

★ Use <u>adjectives</u> to describe the following Geoscience *processes* and *systems*.

(1) Lava Flow	(2) Metamorphism	(3) Foliation
(4) Metasomatism	(5) Crystallization	(6) Rock Cycle

23. Words and Expressions Associated with Geology

Some words are well known today because they are important to the field of geology, which is the study of the Earth's crust, its layers, and its physical history.

★ **Match the word or expression from the Choice Box with the correct meaning of that word.**

1. _____ A vent in the Earth's surface through which molten lava erupts

2. _____ The outer layer of the Earth

3. _____ A rock formation that holds water

4. _____ The slow movements of the continents

5. _____ A region of sandbanks and sandbars formed at the mouth of a river

6. _____ The center portion of the Earth

7. _____ A pile or mound of windblown sand

8. _____ The winding path or bends and loops of a river

9. _____ A slow moving ice or snow block over land

10. _____ The remains of a plant or animal imbedded in rock

11. _____ Where deposits of sediment during times of flood in a river valley are left

12. _____ A large grained igneous rock containing feldspar, quartz, and mica

13. _____ The attractive force of one object to another due to their mass

14. _____ Molten material before it comes to the Earth's surface

15. _____ Molten material that was magma but is now at the Earth's surface

CHOICE BOX

core	glacier	crust	fossil	aquifer
dune	flood plain	gravity	granite	delta
meander	lava	Continental Drift	magma	volcano

NAME _____ DATE _____

24. Geoscience Expressions

★ Find the word or expression that does *not* belong to each group and write it on the space provided.

1. dirt, soil, mud, flowers _____

2. metal, flare, ore, mineral _____

3. Continental drift, tectonics, movement, nebula _____

4. till, caveman, glacier, moraine _____

5. atom, Adam, molecule, electron _____

6. beach, shoreline, pistons, sand _____

7. barometer, thermometer, anemometer, seismometer _____

8. aquifer, hydrology, money, water _____

9. Cambrian, era, epoch, Einstein _____

10. climate, potato, tornado, weather _____

11. conglomerate, fragments, sedimentary, igneous _____

12. Dinosaur, Tyrannosaurus, Triceratops, Tyrannotops _____

13. toast, crust, mantle, core _____

14. crater, dune, sand, desert _____

15. granite, ecology, environment, life cycle _____

16. geyser, groundwater, glacier, Old Faithful _____

17. repel, adhesion, attraction, magnetism _____

18. Ice Age, glacier, ice cream, ice cap _____

19. shortitude, longitude, latitude _____

20. meander, river, bend, loop, straight _____

25. Geoscience Relationships

★   Listed below is a series of Geoscience words or phrases joined by a line. Your task is to place on the line the appropriate letter from the Chart that describes the relationship between the words. Some words or phrases may have more than one letter. You may need a glossary or dictionary. The first one has been completed for you.

CHART

0—opposite	S—same	R—only related	UR—unrelated

1. sun __S__ star
2. slump _____ soil
3. erosion _____ stable platform
4. stalactite _____ stalagmite
5. anticline _____ anticyclone
6. absolute magnitude _____ apparent magnitude
7. buoyancy _____ floating
8. caldera _____ volcano
9. cast _____ fossil
10. cementation _____ conglomerate
11. cirque _____ quark
12. climate _____ weather
13. air _____ vacuum
14. ore _____ mineral
15. oxbow lake _____ cut off meander
16. paleontologist _____ fossil life researcher
17. peat _____ coal
18. penumbra _____ shadow

19. loess _____ shield rock
20. land form _____ topography
21. laccolith _____ intrusive igneous rock
22. luster _____ talc
23. legend _____ directions
24. nucleus _____ center
25. orbit _____ stationary
26. meteorologist _____ meteor researcher
27. Moho _____ Mohorovicic discontinuity
28. nimbus _____ cumulus
29. mass _____ amount of object matter
30. smog _____ smoke and fog
31. thrust _____ rocket
32. equilibrium _____ variance
33. telescope _____ trombone
34. quarry _____ marble

26. Interesting Geoscience Vocabulary Clues

★ Complete the following Geoscience vocabulary words by using the clues given below each one. The first one has been completed for you. A Choice Box has been provided.

1. com__pounds__
   (*weights*)

2. _____ure
   (*iron clothes*)

3. pollut_____
   (*insects*)

4. _____ness
   (*not soft*)

5. _____ralogist
   (*ore shaft*)

6. _____az
   (*not bottom*)

7. tec_____ics
   (*2,000 lbs.*)

8. seismo_____
   (*chart style*)

9. vol_____o
   (*food container*)

10. t_____ami
    (*a star*)

11. _____tle
    (*not lady*)

12. w_____hering
    (*devour*)

13. _____au
    (*round dish*)

14. mag_____
    (*fish trap*)

15. _____ain
    (*ascend*)

16. geo_____y
    (*cut tree*)

17. atmosp_____
    (*not there*)

18. _____ water
    (*not air*)

19. shore_____
    (*rope*)

20. _____ertia
    (*not out*)

21. _____olith
    (*come clean*)

22. _____ancy
    (*sea marker*)

23. hypo_____
    (*college assignment*)

24. _____bon
    (*auto*)

25. _____ness
    (*smart*)

26. _____aeologist
    (*wall opening support*)

27. as_____ospheres
    (*not now*)

28. _____urate
    (*did not stand*)

29. Alpha _____auri
    (*penny*)

30. Precam_____
    (*boy's name*)

CHOICE BOX

sun	thesis	man
here	graph	mount
Cent	plate	line
mine	ground	eat
sat	bath	~~pounds~~
ton	car	bright
press	then	hard
net	log	arch
buoy	can	top
in	ants	brian

27. Double-Decker Fossil Fuels

★ The statements below require a set of two answers to complete them. Choose the set of two answers from the Choice Box on the right. Not all answers in the Choice Box will be used.

1. The growth in _____ and _____ have placed a tremendous demand on the supply of fossil fuels.

2. Fossil fuels result from the decay of _____ and _____.

3. _____ and _____ are two forms of coal.

4. Coal is formed under great _____ and _____ in the Earth.

5. Two early stages of coal are _____ and _____.

6. Petroleum is made of two elements called _____ and _____.

7. When petroleum is refined, it separates into different substances such as _____ and _____.

8. _____ and _____ are normally found in the same oil pool or deposit.

9. _____ and _____ are two major industrial consumers of fossil fuels.

10. _____ and _____ are two ways we can lessen our dependence on fossil fuels.

CHOICE BOX

heat, pressure

cool, freezing

gasoline, kerosene

black, green

oil, natural gas

Bruins, Rangers

bituminous, anthracite

Pistons, Celtics

manufacturing, transportation

population, consumption

peat, lignite

muscle, firewood

plants, animals

reducing, recycling

hydrogen, carbon

report, reply

reject, report

28. A Crusty Puzzle

★ Study the descriptions of the Earth's crust. Then choose the correct answer from the Choice Box.

1. Name given to the resulting break after rock movement on either side of a fracture in the Earth's crust.

2. The boundary line between crust and mantle is defined by the _____ discontinuity.

3. The _____ is directly below the Earth's crust.

4. The name of the outermost layer of the Earth's crust and upper mantle.

5. This type of action occurs at the crust's surface.

6. The Earth's crust is studied by use of _____ waves.

7. The continental crust is _____ than the ocean crust.

8. The upper continental crust consists of _____ rocks.

9. Strata of rock walls can reveal the _____ of the crust.

10. The top layer of ocean crust consists of _____ muds.

CHOICE BOX

age	volcanic	sedimentary	lithosphere	thicker
shock	igneous	Mohorovicic	fault	mantle

SECTION 2

ESSENTIAL STRATEGIES FOR THE SCIENTIFIC METHOD

LEARNING

NAME _____   DATE _____

29. The Scientific Method

★ Find the word from the Choice Box that should appear in each numbered blank located in the paragraphs on the right. Write the correct word for the numbered blank on the left. No word may be used more than once.

QUICK ACCESS
information

1. _Scientists_
2. _granted_
3. _?_
4. _why_
5. _blue_
6. _reflects_
7. _?_
8. _problems_
9. _theories_
10. _method_
11. _flaws_
12. _data_
13. _experiements_
14. _thinking_
15. _hypothesis_
16. _work_
17. _fourth_
18. _test_
19. _corrections_
20. _abandoned_

Many __1__ do not look at life events or processes the same way people who take things for __2__ do. These scientists have what is called "an investigative __3__" or an investigative point of view. These people enjoy looking at the "__4__" of things. For example, a scientist will not just say, "The sky is __5__ today." She/He will think the sky is blue today because the atmosphere __6__ the blue end of the spectrum. These people are __7__ and investigate __8__ by using the scientific method.

In the first step of the scientific method, the scientist looks at and studies all the available data, the facts, and __9__ about a problem.

The scientist then goes to the second step in the scientific __10__, which is to search for __11__ or errors in the __12__ collected on a problem. The second step or search may include a series of __13__ or a mental exercise of logical deductive reasoning or __14__.

The third step in the scientific method is to develop a new __15__ (an educated assumption or explanation) to help clarify the problem if the old ideas are incorrect, flawed, or don't __16__ as they should.

The __17__ step in the scientific method is to __18__ the new hypothesis in every way possible and make the necessary __19__. In this fourth step, the hypothesis may be __20__ if it does not hold up under investigation.

CHOICE BOX

granted	scientists	test	experiments	thinking
why	theories	method	hypothesis	problem
reflects	flaws	inquisitive	corrections	paradigm
abandoned	fourth	data	work	blue

30. Scientific Method Expressions

★ Using all the letter pairs in the Choice Box, fill in the answers to the clues about scientific method expressions.

CHOICE BOX

ED	RO	EN	DI	~~PO~~	SE	RI	~~EM~~	CE
ED	EV	UR	OC	EP	OB	LE	PP	~~IS~~
IN	~~RE~~	NC	PR	RT	~~EX~~	~~TH~~	AB	ME
RI	TI	~~NT~~	ES					

CLUE

1. Educated guess
2. Test
3. Needs solving
4. A foretelling of results
5. Observable clues
6. Idea
7. Receive reinforcement
8. To redo better
9. Forces affecting experiments
10. To prove wrong
11. Processes
12. Calculating amounts

ANSWER GRID

H	Y	P	O	T	H	E	S	I	S
E	X	P	E	R	E	M	E	N	T
P	R	O	B	L	E	M			
				I	C			O	N
		I	D						
C	O					T			
S	U		O						
		V	I						
V	A							S	
		S	P			V	E		
P	R					U	R		
		A	S				G		

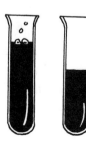

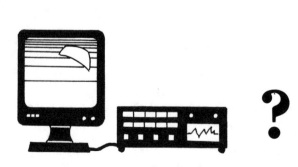

31. Scientific Method Expressions from Clues and Scrambles

★ The descriptions in Column 1 are clues to finding the scientific method word you need for Column 3. Column 2 is the word you need for Column 3; however, it is scrambled. Place the unscrambled answer in Column 3.

Column 1—Clues	Column 2	Column 3
1. An idea about something	RHEOTY	_ _ _ _ _ _
2. The test of a process by comparing and control	NPRMTIEXEE	_ _ _ _ _ _ _ _ _ _
3. Scientists search for this	HTRTU	_ _ _ _ _
4. Leaving an idea that does not work	AADNNGIONB	_ _ _ _ _ _ _ _ _
5. What you start with	RBEPMLO	_ _ _ _ _ _ _
6. Scientists ask this	YHW	_ _ _
7. Scientists ask this	WOH	_ _ _
8. Another name for facts	ATAD	_ _ _ _
9. An imitation substance used in experiments	LCBPAEO	_ _ _ _ _ _ _
10. The outcome of an experiment	EUTSLSR	_ _ _ _ _ _ _
11. Science must be this to not exchange wishes for facts	CTBOIVEJE	_ _ _ _ _ _ _ _ _
12. Similar experiments must give these results	MASE	_ _ _ _
13. This means to look into things	NUEIRIQ	_ _ _ _ _ _ _
14. The science of machines	CHOLTENOGY	_ _ _ _ _ _ _ _ _ _
15. A way of getting facts	NOITAVRESBO	_ _ _ _ _ _ _ _ _ _ _

32. Science Skill Enhancement

★ Here is an exercise designed to sharpen your knowledge of science skills. Each statement is referring to a science skill in the Choice Box. Write the correct science skill next to each statement.

1. Bighampton saw the arachnids crawling toward him.
   _____

2. "Let's put all the large black ones in a beaker and the small white ones in a box," he said. _____

3. "I bet those spiders will bite," Sonia stated.
   _____

4. "They must be going ten miles an hour," Akira blurted.
   _____

5. "If they are that fast, they must be able to run after insects," Sonia mused. _____

6. "I have an idea," Akira stated. "All spiders that run after their prey don't need webs." _____

7. Akira said, "My ruler shows this one to be half an inch wide." _____

8. "I placed all the spider data on my computer," Bighampton revealed. _____

CHOICE BOX

classifying

hypothesizing

observing

estimating

measuring

predicting

inferring

recording

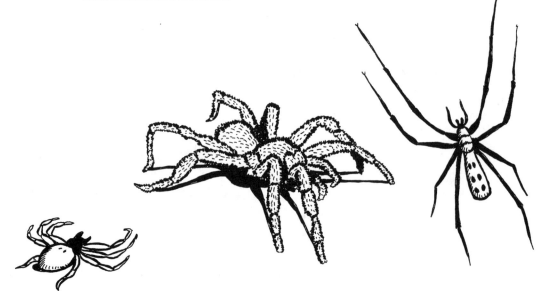

33. Scientific Method Reverse Questions

★ Here is a reversal of sorts. You are given the answers to a series of questions regarding the scientific method or scientific inquiry. Your task is to make an intelligent question that would be suitable for each answer.

1. An hypothesis is an educated guess, a proposed assumption, an assertion to be worked through.

   _____

   _____

2. Scientists cannot conduct proper experiments if they have a bias or are not open minded.

   _____

   _____

3. Scientists must verify their hypotheses by testing.

   _____

   _____

4. You can design an experiment to prove your hypothesis to be wrong.

   _____

   _____

5. The first thing a scientist does is to identify the problem to be solved.

   _____

   _____

6. If a prediction about the results of an experiment is untrue, the concept is discarded, disproved, or modified.

   _____

   _____

7. Out of a thousand positive-result experiments, one false result will void the hypothesis.

   _____

   _____

8. When you design an experiment, you seek to control and identify the variables as well as set out the processes and procedures of the experiment.

   _____

   _____

34. Francis Bacon: Hypothesis and Scientific Inquiry

QUICK ACCESS information

★ Pick the word from the Choice Box that should appear in the numbered blank in the following paragraphs. Write your answers on the numbered blanks on the left.

1. _____
2. _____
3. _____
4. _____
5. _____
6. _____
7. _____
8. _____
9. _____
10. _____
11. _____
12. _____
13. _____
14. _____
15. _____
16. _____
17. _____
18. _____
19. _____
20. _____

Francis Bacon, in the early 1600s, was a __1__ in the area of __2__ inquiry. He wanted to __3__ data for experiments in an __4__ minded way. He would often __5__ a hypothesis, which is an __6__ guess or a proposed assumption by __7__ and trying to __8__ the __9__.

Francis Bacon ran a series of tests on the __10__ by __11__. If the experiments __12__ the hypothesis to be true, then the hypothesis became a scientific __13__, which was __14__ in journals so other scientists could use the law. The name "Scientific Induction" has been given to the __15__ by which Francis Bacon formulated his hypothesis.

As time passed, other scientists __16__ Francis Bacon's process of __17__ to the extent that now a hypothesis may not be a __18__ law. It is kept only as long as it __19__ with new scientific work and observations. If it __20__ to agree, it is then retested and discarded and a new hypothesis formed.

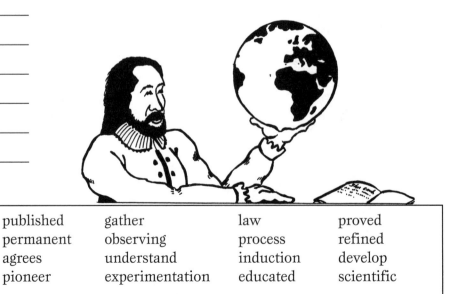

CHOICE BOX

open	published	gather	law	proved
data	permanent	observing	process	refined
fails	agrees	understand	induction	develop
hypothesis	pioneer	experimentation	educated	scientific

35. A Group Research Project: Part One

★ Worksheets 35, 36, and 37 outline a group research project. Each group is to develop a specific topic and present its findings to the class.

Topic _____

Date Due _____

Participants (alphabetical order) _____

_____

Recorder _____

Getting Started:

Describe the topic. (Written by the designated recorder)

_____

_____

_____

_____

_____

_____

Present knowledge before research—best found by brainstorming. Remember brainstorming rule: All ideas are valid and cannot be criticized, evaluated, or questioned at this time.

_____

_____

_____

_____

_____

Give vocabulary relative to the topic. _____

_____

_____

36. A Group Research Project: Part Two

The Questions: List a series of questions about your topic for which you do not have an answer at this time. Each person in the group is to contribute at least one question. (*Optional*: Place the name of the group member beside the question each has contributed.)

_____

_____

_____

_____

_____

The Sources: List the sources you need to contact for information on your topic.

_____

_____

_____

_____

Contact Method: How are "sources of resources" going to be contacted? Which group members are responsible for collecting research in which areas of the topic?

How?_____

_____

_____

_____

Who does what?_____

_____

_____

_____

_____

_____

(Remember the bibliography format that must be followed.)

37. A Group Research Project: Part Three

Organization: What method is used to organize and present material?

_____

_____

Resources List (*Optional*: Place the name of the group member beside the resource each has found.)

_____

_____

_____

_____

Question Review: Are your earlier questions (see Part Two) still valid? Add any new questions at this time.

_____

_____

_____

_____

The Presentation Rules:

1. Organize presentation beforehand.

2. Give presentation in chronological (common sense) order.

3. Be sure speaker is clear, concise, and interesting.

4. If allowed, use audio/visuals, charts, and diagrams.

5. If more than one speaker, be sure each has distinct responsibility for each area of the presentation. Avoid overlapping.

6. Involve your whole group if possible.

7. Decide ahead of time if audience participation is to take place. If so, support may be needed to help presenters.

Evaluation Method: To be determined by teacher or decided upon by group members.

_____

_____

38. Safety in the Science Lab: Part One

★ Choose the correct word or phrase at the end of each sentence that best completes the sentence. Be sure to keep worksheets 38, 39, 40, and 41 in your science notebook.

A. GENERAL SAFETY IDEAS

1. Students must _____ jostling, roughhousing, or negative attitude behavior while in the lab. **(avoid, agree with, pay no attention to)**

2. Never work without a _____.
   (weigh scale, partner, Bunsen burner)

3. Keep yourself free from _____. Do not wear baggy clothing, dangling jewelry, or long hair that can be caught in the apparatus of an experiment. **(cigarettes, money, clutter)**

4. Inform the teacher or lab assistant if you wear _____ lenses.
   (monofocal, contact, bifocal)

5. _____ the teacher aware of any medical problems such as allergies or conditions that need accommodations. **(Make, Aware, Telephone)**

6. Thomas Edison performed experiments outside the school. At one point, he caused a fire on a train. You are not to perform any experiment _____ the school. **(outside, beside, inside)**

7. The science lab is _____ place for food or drinks. **(the, no, secret)**

8. Do not _____ anything in the science lab, not even your lunch at noon. **(yell, borrow, eat)**

9. Do not put your _____ to your mouth, eyes, or nose when working in a science lab. **(hand, toe, ear)**

10. Do not _____ anything to another student in the science lab.
    (lend, catch, throw)

11. Report any injury or burn to the teacher _____.
    (immediately, now and then, occasionally)

12. Check your lab/work area to make sure all equipment is _____.
    (operational, usual, defunct)

39. Safety in the Science Lab: Part Two

★ Choose the correct word or phrase at the end of each sentence that best completes the meaning of the sentence. Be sure to keep worksheets 38, 39, 40, and 41 in your science notebook.

B. WORKING WITH MATERIALS

1. Do not take anything from the lab without _____.
   (authorization, specification, deduction)

2. When required to smell a substance, use your hand to waft the odor toward you. Do not _____ smell the contents of a container.
   (quietly, surely, directly)

3. Dispose of harmful chemicals only in the method your teacher _____. **(instructs, challenges, guesses)**

4. If you or your partner has a _____ with chemicals, first ask your teacher's advice, then totally clean the area. **(mishap, fun, horse)**

5. When necessary wear safety goggles, gloves, _____, and lab coats.
   (T-shirts, fan belts, aprons)

6. Use utmost care when _____ with lab animals.
   (working, playing, petting)

7. Use utmost _____ when using a dissecting blade, probe, or cutting tool. **(care, share, snare)**

8. Wash your _____ after any session in the lab.
   (bands, plans, hands)

9. If part of your body _____ a toxic substance, immediately ask for instruction from the teacher, as not all chemicals can be washed off.
   (reaches, bleaches, touches)

10. When _____ one substance into another, keep your face and other exposed areas away from the process. **(leaning, pouring, heaving)**

11. Learn which chemical substances react _____ with other substances. **(violently, nicely, closely)**

12. If you feel a substance or material is making you _____, tell the teacher immediately. **(ill, blue, Canadian)**

40. Safety in the Science Lab: Part Three

★ Choose the correct word or phrase at the end of each sentence that best completes the meaning of the sentence. Be sure to keep worksheets 38, 39, 40, and 41 in your science notebook.

C. WORKING WITH HEAT AND COLD

1. Touching dry ice can _____freeze_____ your skin solid faster than fire can burn it. **(enhance, freeze, tan)**

2. When performing an experiment or observing data outside in the _____winter_____, remember that metal objects will stick to your tongue and cause severe, painful injury. **(winter, summer, spring)**

3. An electric hot plate is always _____safer_____ than an open flame. **(younger, older, safer)**

4. Hot plates must be turned off and unplugged _____after_____ use. **(before, after, during)**

5. Ask the teacher which beakers or containers are heat _____friendly_____. Only use these for heating. **(resistant, friendly, useful)**

6. _____Watch_____ for over-boiling or boiling dry. **(Decide, Locate, Watch)**

7. The _____open_____ end of test tubes should be pointed away from experimenters and observers. **(open, dead, both)**

8. A test tube can be _____heated_____ in water in a heat-resistant beaker. However, care must be taken to dispose of the hot or boiling water in the beaker after use. **(curled, heated, wasted)**

9. Hot objects are best picked up with _____?_____. **(tongs, prongs, gongs)**

10. Old heating equipment can have flaws. You must report any malfunction or "near" broken part to the teacher. Do not use _____faulty_____ equipment, even if it can be "made" to work. **(faulty, pretty, green)**

11. Follow the school's shutdown _____procedure_____, extinguish all flames, unplug all hot plates, and secure any flame source (matches) at the end of use. **(style, procedure, calling)**

41. Safety in the Science Lab: Part Four

★ Choose the correct word or phrase at the end of each sentence that best completes the meaning of the sentence. Be sure to keep worksheets 38, 39, 40, and 41 in your science notebook.

D. EQUIPMENT SAFETY

1. Follow the Bunsen burner safety _____ in the following areas. **(speculation, procedure, run around)**

   a. Read the instructions for understanding.
   b. Keep flammables (like contact cement) away from flame.
   c. Use with authorization only.
   d. Do not leave an open flame unattended.
   e. Use the correct lighting procedure.
   f. Do not lean over an open flame.

2. Check the nozzle of a Bunsen burner before use for debris from _____ users. **(new, tired, previous)**

3. Make sure all _____ objects used in the lab are free from cracks or flaws. **(glass, wet, blue)**

4. Even a balance _____ can be dangerous. Make sure it or other heavier objects are secure in your work area. **(scale, beam, act)**

5. _____ rods and tubing can shatter easily. Do not put undue stress on these. **(Steel, Carbon, Glass)**

6. When sharing equipment, be _____ of the safety needs of the other person(s). **(envious, scared, aware)**

7. Follow your school's _____-up procedure after all experiments. **(clean, beam, green)**

8. If you cut your hand with a piece of lab equipment, don't put the bloodied part into your _____. **(mouth, shoe, glove)**

9. Do not _____ water pistols, rubber bands, or pea or spitball shooters into the lab. **(bring, create, drive)**

10. Do not _____ a rubber stopper or glass rod into a stopper while the beaker is being heated. **(rub, insert, invent)**

42. The Great Search for Science "In" Words

★ Many of the words associated with science and the scientific method begin with the two letters "in." Pick the "in" word from the Choice Box that fits each definition.

1. _____ a bright hot light invented by Edison

2. _____ not alive

3. _____ not accurate

4. _____ something that cannot be heard

5. _____ to ask or seek out

6. _____ to burn to ashes

7. _____ a cut made when dissecting a frog

8. _____ to slant or slope

9. _____ not understood; disconnected speech

10. _____ not able to put one thing with another

11. _____ a lack of agreement

12. _____ having no importance

13. _____ not the same results every time

14. _____ the wrong results

15. _____ a device to keep things (eggs) warm and environmentally secure

16. _____ not able to be cured

17. _____ to cause to happen; to lead on or persuade

18. _____ process by which electrical or magnetic properties are transferred to a nearby object

19. _____ resulting from productive labor or manufacturing

20. _____ the tendency of a still object to remain still or a moving object to continue moving in the same direction unless acted upon by some outside force

Incredible!

Copyright © 2003 by John Wiley & Sons, Inc.

CHOICE BOX

inanimate	incline	incorrect	incandescent	incoherence
inaccurate	incurable	incubator	induction	inertia
inconsequential	inconsistent	incongruence	incision	incinerate
induce	inaudible	incompatible	inquire	industry

43. Researching B.C.E. Scientific Thinkers

★ Listed below are a series of accomplishments of B.C.E. (Before Common Era) scientific thinkers. Your task is to write the name of the scientist responsible for each accomplishment at the end of each statement. (Each person's years are given merely for your information.) A Choice Box has been provided. Each answer is used more than once. You may need a resource such as an encyclopedia.

1. He is known as "The Father of Modern Medicine." _____

2. He concluded the Earth was spherical. _____

3. He calculated the size of the Earth. _____

4. He reasoned that the sun must be curved. _____

5. He formulated a principle of buoyancy. _____

6. He was a Greek thinker who is often called the first great biologist.

_____

7. He taught Alexander the Great. _____

8. Graduating medical students take an oath named after this person.

_____

9. He defined the value of pi (3.14) used to find the perimeter and area of circles.

_____

10. He performed early surgery and used tar as an antiseptic. _____

11. He developed a screw-type pump and a war catapult. _____

12. He reasoned that all substances were mixtures of earth, fire, air, and water.

_____

CHOICE BOX

Hippocrates	Aristotle	Archimedes	Erastoshenes
(460–*c.* 377 B.C.)	(384–322 B.C.)	(287–212 B.C.)	(275–*c.* 195 B.C.)

44. Finding Pre-1900 Scientists from Clues and Scrambles

★ Listed in Column 1 are the accomplishments of a number of famous pre-1900 scientists. In Column 2 are the names you need for Column 3; however, they are scrambled. Using the clues and scrambles, place the correct answers in Column 3.

Column 1	Column 2	Column 3
1. He performed skull surgery around 390 B.C.	TPRAPHIOECS	_ _ _ _ _ _ _ _ _ _
2. This Greek philosopher was considered to be the first great biologist.	RSLETAOTI	_ _ _ _ _ _ _ _
3. In the 1600s, he used the experimental method to confirm theories.	BCNOA	_ _ _ _ _
4. He developed the theory that the Earth is a planet that revolves around the sun.	ORCCINUPSE	_ _ _ _ _ _ _ _ _ _
5. He helped solidify the scientific method. He also improved the telescope.	AOELLGI	_ _ _ _ _ _ _
6. He developed the laws of planetary motion.	ELREKP	_ _ _ _ _ _
7. He published a major work on the body's heart/blood system.	AVYHER	_ _ _ _ _ _
8. He formulated laws on gravity and motion.	ETOWNN	_ _ _ _ _ _
9. He predicted the appearance of the comet that bears his name.	AEHYLL	_ _ _ _ _ _
10. He discovered the planet Uranus.	EHRHSCEL	_ _ _ _ _ _ _ _
11. He developed the theory of pasteurization.	ASPERUT	_ _ _ _ _ _ _
12. He discovered x-rays.	NETORNEG	_ _ _ _ _ _ _ _

45. Finding Post-1900 Scientists from Clues and Scrambles

★ Listed in Column 1 are the accomplishments of a number of famous scientists. In Column 2 are the names you need for Column 3; however, they are scrambled. Using the clues and scrambles, place the correct answers in Column 3.

$$E = MC^2$$

Column 1	Column 2	Column 3
1. She made fundamental discoveries in the field of radiation.	RICUE	_ _ _ _ _
2. He developed the General Theory of Relativity.	IEITENNS	_ _ _ _ _ _ _ _
3. He developed radar.	AONWTS	_ _ _ _ _ _
4. He developed a variety of uses for U.S. agricultural crops, especially soybeans, sweet potatoes, and peanuts.	RRVCAE	_ _ _ _ _ _
5. These two Canadians discovered insulin for the treatment of diabetes.	TESB & ABNGNTI	_ _ _ _ & _ _ _ _ _ _
6. He discovered penicillin.	LIGNFME	_ _ _ _ _ _ _
7. He detected radio waves beyond our Solar System.	ASYKJN	_ _ _ _ _ _
8. He showed that genes consist of DNA.	ERVYA	_ _ _ _ _
9. He revealed the development of a polio vaccine.	AKSL	_ _ _ _
10. He was the first person to orbit the Earth.	AGRGAIN	_ _ _ _ _ _ _
11. She published *Silent Spring*, making people aware of pollution.	ROCNSA	_ _ _ _ _ _
12. He was the first person to set foot on the moon.	ARSRNGOTM	_ _ _ _ _ _ _ _ _

46. The Hypothesis Concept

★ Find a word from the Choice Box that should appear in each numbered blank located in the paragraphs on the right. Write the correct word on the left.

1. _____

2. _____

3. _____

4. _____

5. _____

6. _____

7. _____

8. _____

9. _____

10. _____

11. _____

12. _____

13. _____

14. _____

15. _____

16. _____

17. _____

18. _____

19. _____

20. _____

Central to understanding the __1__, techniques, and ideas that are the __2__ of the Scientific __3__ is the concept of the hypothesis. The __4__ tells us that "to form a hypothesis" about a __5__ or problem, you __6__ a supposition or a __7__ assumption as a basis for __8__. This is fine, but what does it mean?

The term "to form a hypothesis" means you make an educated __9__ or present an informed __10__ about the reason the problem __11__ or occurs. In order to __12__ educated to make that guess or informed to make that explanation, two things must __13__. First, the situation or problem must be stated __14__. Second, you must __15__ observable data on the situation or __16__.

This data will eventually __17__ in the __18__ of the educated guess/hypothesis/informed explanation by __19__. When the hypothesis is supported by positive testing, this will often lead to a __20__ about the problem or situation.

CHOICE BOX

collect	explanation	Method	make	testing
guess	occur	clearly	theory	proposed
core	situation	exists	reasoning	problem
experimentation	help	become	processes	dictionary

47. The Science Career Graph: Part One

★ Read the graph below. Then answer the related questions on this page and the next page.

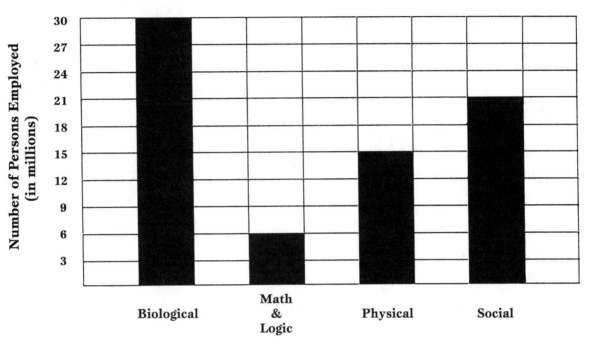

1. What is the meaning of the bars on the graph?

_____

_____

_____

2. What can you infer from the fact that the first bar on the graph is the longest, yet there is a large drop to the second bar?

_____

_____

_____

3. How many people are in the largest group? _____

4. Which group has the fewest number of people? _____

48. The Science Career Graph: Part Two

5. If 30% of the people in Social Sciences were social workers, how many people would this be? _____

6. In the field of Biological Science, 65% of the people are in health care. How many people would this be? _____

7. How many more people work in the field of Social Sciences than in the field of Physical Sciences? _____

8. In the Physical Sciences, the areas of Engineering, Chemistry, Electronics, and Physics take up 40% of the careers. How many people work in the remaining areas in the field of Physical Sciences? _____

9. The field of Math & Logic is a small but growing area of work. If it grows by 2 million people next year, how many people will be working in this area at that time? _____

10. What is the total number of people working in all the fields of science according to the graph? _____

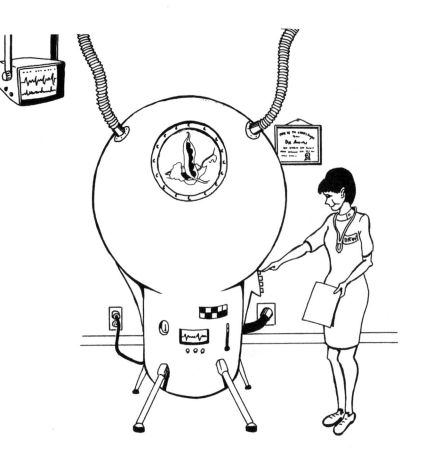

49. Think About It

★ **The following are some "old-fashioned" views of the Earth. Describe in a sentence why you think these old-fashioned ideas may or may not be correct.**

1. The Earth is flat.

   _____

   _____

   _____

2. Apollo, the god of the Sun, let his son race his chariot over the sky, causing ice caps, deserts, and large cracks in the Earth's surface.

   _____

   _____

   _____

3. The sun and moon revolve around the Earth.

   _____

   _____

   _____

4. A volcano can be made to stop erupting by throwing a sacrifice into its mouth and thereby satisfying it.

   _____

   _____

   _____

5. The human body while on Earth cannot travel faster than 15 miles per hour.

   _____

   _____

   _____

6. Astrology is a science.

   _____

   _____

   _____

50. A Scientific Method Scramble

★ As you read the explanation of the scientific method in the paragraph at the right, unscramble the letters in each blank to form the word that completes the statement. Write the word correctly in the corresponding numbered space on the left. A Choice Box has been provided.

1. _____

2. _____

3. _____

4. _____

5. _____

6. _____

7. _____

8. _____

9. _____

10. _____

11. _____

12. _____

13. _____

14. _____

15. _____

The Scientific Method is the (1) SATICMYSTE method or process used by (2) SCETSTINTIS to solve (3) RBESMLOP. The problem being dealt with is put through a complete (4) NXAIAIOTNME and (5) INSIAIONTGTEV by using (6) ASRCHEER and (7) OWLEGDNKE available at the time. The (8) OSTIEVPI or (9) TIVEAGNE results are (10) TDESDIU and made into a proposition assumed as a basis for (11) NINGOEARS, better known as an (12) POTHYHESIS. The hypothesis is then put through a thorough (13) RIFICOITAVEN process using experiments, (14) EVIDEDUCT reasoning, and (15) VATIONREOBS.

CHOICE BOX

scientists	hypothesis	studied	systematic	knowledge
verification	problems	reasoning	research	deductive
positive	investigation	examination	negative	observation

SECTION 3

REVOLVING AND ROTATING WITH THE SOLAR SYSTEM

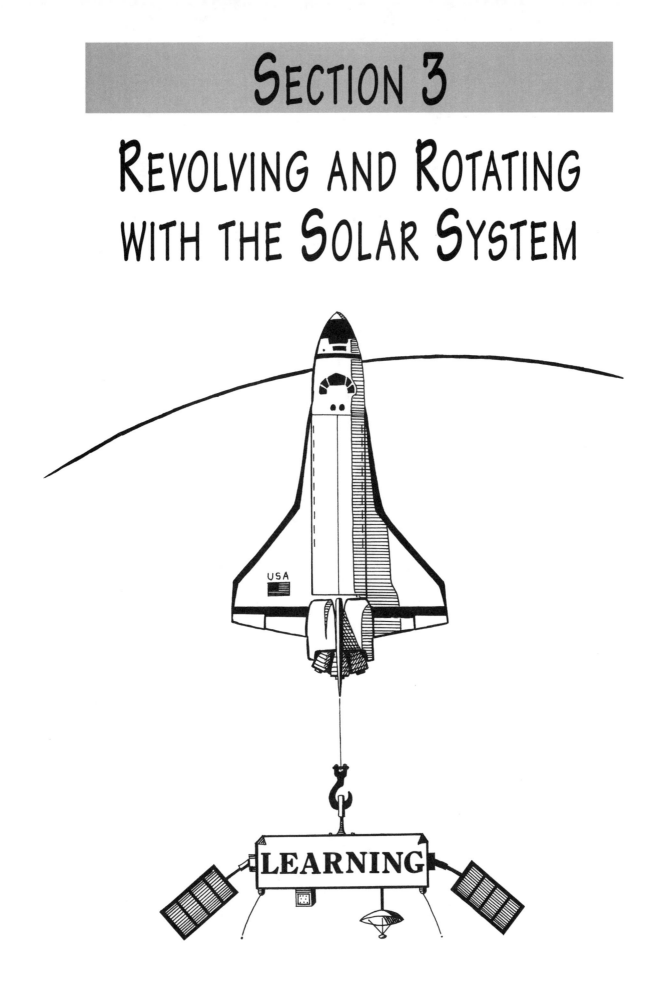

LEARNING

51. Pioneers of Astronomy, Rocketry, and Space Flight: Part One

★ Read the clues below to reveal the names of astronomy, rocketry, and space flight pioneers. Place their names in the appropriate locations on the puzzle. A Choice Box has been provided.

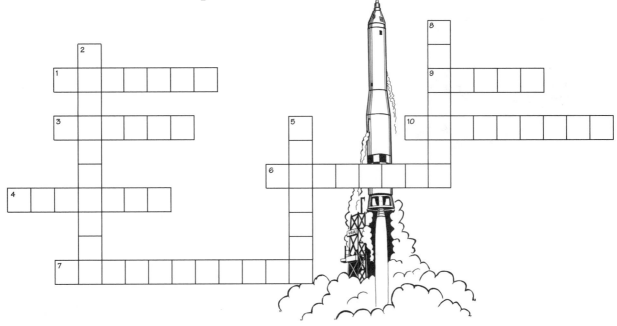

1. He was a 1903 American rocket scientist.

2. He first believed the planets revolved around the sun, not the Earth.

3. He discovered the elliptical orbits of planets.

4. He improved the telescope to study the stars and planets.

5. In Alexandria, Egypt, he mapped planets and developed theories of their movements.

6. He was a German rocket scientist who came to the U.S. after World War II.

7. He was a Russian school teacher who developed rocket ideas in 1895.

8. He was the first person to be rocketed into orbit around the Earth.

9. He was the first American to orbit the Earth.

10. He was the first person to set foot on the moon's surface.

CHOICE BOX

Copernicus	Goddard	Tsiolkovsky	Armstrong	Galileo
Glenn	Gagarin	Ptolemy	Kepler	Von Braun

52. Pioneers of Astronomy, Rocketry, and Space Flight: Part Two

★   Read the clues below to reveal the names of astronomy, rocketry, and space flight pioneers. Place their names in the appropriate locations in the puzzle. A Choice Box has been provided.

1. This person developed a huge reflecting telescope in 1789.

2. This Dutch spectacle maker developed the first telescope.

3. She found the periods of cepheid stars are directly related to their brightness.

4. This genius developed the Principle of Universal Gravitation.

5. This U.S. astronomer showed that galaxies are receding. A space telescope is named after him.

6. He developed the "General Theory of Relativity" in 1916.

7. This person made the first known detailed chart of the stars' positions.

8. This person discovered the two moons of Mars and calculated their orbits in 1877.

9. The name of the second person to set foot on the moon.

10. This person speculated that Mars was covered with irrigation canals to bring water from frozen polar ice caps. An observatory in Flagstaff, Arizona, is named after him.

CHOICE BOX

Hubble	Einstein	Lippershey	Hipparchus	Swan
Hall	Herschel	Newton	Aldrin	Lowell

NAME _____ DATE _____

53. Solar System "Things in Common"

★ Listed below are sets of words, phrases, or people from science. Your task is to tell what each set of things, phrases, or people have in common by answering with "Things that . . .," "People who . . .," or "Planets that . . . ." The first one has been completed for you.

1. Earth, asteroids, Uranus: ___Things that can revolve around our sun___

2. Robert Goddard, Werner Von Braun: _____

3. 24-hour rotation, life, 365-day rotation: _____

4. tide, eclipse, Sea of Tranquillity: _____

5. Mercury, Venus, Earth, Mars: _____

6. corona, sunspots, solar flare: _____

7. Jupiter, Saturn, Uranus, Neptune, Pluto: _____

8. red, Phobos and Demos, ½ Earth diameter: _____

9. between Mars and Jupiter, meteorites, cosmic fragments: _____

_____

10. over twice Earth's gravity, red spot, 16 moons: _____

11. Apollo 11, space shuttle, pioneer space probes: _____

_____

12. Copernicus, Kepler, Galileo: _____

59

54. Solar System Adjectives

In the study of Earth Science, we look at many things, processes, and systems that can be better understood if we can describe aspects of each one.

★   Use <u>adjectives</u> to describe the following *things* of the Solar System.

(1) Sun	(2) Earth	(3) Jupiter
(4) Meteorites	(5) Comets	(6) Sunspots

★   Use <u>adjectives</u> to describe the following *processes* and *systems* of the Solar System.

(1) Orbits	(2) Gravity	(3) Eclipse
(4) Weightlessness	(5) Rotation	(6) Revolution

55. Solar System Search from Clues

★ The partially spelled Solar System words, phrases, and terms below are related to or defined by the clue under each one. Your task is to complete the word, phrase, or term using the clues. A Choice Box has been provided.

1. __ U __
   (*the center of our Solar System*)

2. E __ RT __
   (*third planet from the sun*)

3. __ __ P __ __ __ __
   (*the largest planet in our Solar System*)

4. __ __ __ ER __ __ __ __
   (*revolve around the sun in a belt*)

5. __ __ __ __ __ N
   (*this planet has rings*)

6. M __ __ __
   (*this is the red planet*)

7. S __ __ AR   F __ __ __ __ __
   (*bright areas near sunspots*)

8. __ __ R __ __ __ __
   (*the planet closest to the sun*)

9. __ X __ __
   (*what planets rotate on*)

10. __ E __ __ __
    (*the second planet from the sun*)

11. C __ __ __ __ __
    (*mass of cosmic dust and ice*)

12. __ __ T __ __ __ __
    (*these are meteoroids that reach our atmosphere*)

13. __ENT__I__U__ __ __   __ __ __ __E
    (*force throwing a body outward from center of rotation*)

14. P__ RIH __ __ __ __ __
    (*the point when a planet is nearest the sun*)

15. __ H __ __ __ S __ __ __ __ __
    (*the surface of the sun*)

16. __ __ __ __ TE __
    (*this is caused when a meteor impacts the Earth or moon*)

17. R __ __ __ __ __ __
    (*what a planet does around its axis*)

18. __ __ NS __ __ __ __
    (*dark areas on the sun's surface*)

19. __ O __ __
    (*our natural satellite*)

20. __ A __ __ __ __ O
    (*he first used the telescope to observe planets*)

21. __ R __ __ __
    (*the path followed around an object*)

22. __ __ __ __ MB __ __
    (*partial shadow on each side of an eclipse*)

23. __ E __ __ __ G __ __ __ __
    MO __ __ __ __
    (*clockwise movement*)

24. __ __ TELL __ __ __
    (*an object in orbit*)

25. __ __ D __ __
    (*water movements caused by the moon*)

CHOICE BOX

RETROGRADE MOTION	PENUMBRA	ROTATE	TIDES	SATURN
PHOTOSPHERE	PERIHELION	COMETS	AXIS	ASTEROIDS
CENTRIFUGAL FORCE	JUPITER	MERCURY	VENUS	EARTH
SOLAR FLARES	METEORS	MARS	CRATER	SUN
SATELLITE	SUNSPOTS	MOON	ORBIT	GALILEO

56. Solar System "Same As" Vocabulary

★ Many things in the Solar System have similarities, even though at first they may appear to be very different. Your task is to describe how item (A) is somehow like the second item (B). Be sure to use complete, proper sentences for your answers.

1. (A)   Mars   (B)   Earth

_____

_____

2. (A)   Sun   (B)   Moon

_____

_____

3. (A)   Comet   (B)   Meteor

_____

_____

4. (A)   Umbra   (B)   Penumbra

_____

_____

5. (A)   Sunspots   (B)   Solar Flares

_____

_____

6. (A)   Moon Craters   (B)   Moon Maria

_____

_____

7. (A)   Our Moon   (B)   Phobos (Mars's Moon)

_____

_____

8. (A)   Inner Planets   (B)   Outer Planets

_____

_____

57. How One Solar System Object or Event Is <u>Not</u> Like Another

★   Many things in our Solar System have differences, even though at first glance they may appear to be the same. Your task is to describe in a complete, proper sentence how the first item in each line is different from the second item.

1. asteroid, comet _____

   _____

2. perihelion, aphelion _____

   _____

3. weight, mass _____

   _____

4. photosphere, chromosphere _____

   _____

5. longitude, latitude _____

   _____

6. oblate spheroid, sphere _____

   _____

7. hypothesis, theory _____

   _____

8. nebula, nova _____

   _____

9. rotation, revolution _____

   _____

10. meteors, meteoroids _____

   _____

58. Solar System Newspaper Headlines

★ Here are two unusual newspaper headlines. Each one describes some sort of unusual situation. Your task is to write the rest of the newspaper story in the space provided. (You may continue on another sheet of paper, if necessary.) Include as many scientific details as possible.

HUGE METEORITE HEADED FOR EARTH—3 DAYS LEFT

_____

_____

_____

_____

_____

_____

_____

_____

TWO COMETS DISCOVERED TO BE ON A COLLISION COURSE— SPECTACULAR LIGHT SHOW EXPECTED

_____

_____

_____

_____

_____

_____

_____

59. Solar System Tripod Connections

★   Listed below are 14 sets of three words that all have something in common in the study of the Solar System. Identify what they have in common and write your answer in the space provided. A dictionary or glossary will help.

1. Galileo   magnification   aperture   _____

2. shadow   penumbra   umbra   _____

3. planetesimals   asteroids   meteoroids   _____

4. magnetic field   center   heat   _____

5. chromosphere   corona   prominence   _____

6. solar flare   dark region   11-year cycle   _____

7. Mars   Earth   Mercury   _____

8. Luna 1   Explorer 3   Pioneer 4   _____
    (1959)   (1958)   (1959)

9. Van Braun   Goddard   Tsiolkovsky   _____

10. Callisto   Phobus   Deimos   _____

11. Encke's   Halley's   Kohoutek's   _____

12. Uranus   Neptune   Jupiter   _____

13. largest planet   16 moons   red spot   _____

14. life   3rd planet   1 moon   _____

60. Solar System Vocabulary Vowelless Puzzle

★ Listed in the Choice Box are some of the most important words associated with our Solar System. Your task is to find and circle the correct Solar System words in the puzzle. All of the vowels (A, E, I, O, U, Y) have been removed. You will need to write the vowels in place as you find the words.

CHOICE BOX

PHOTOSPHERE	AURORA	METEOR	DEIMOS	APOGEE
CORONA	SUNSPOT	ASTEROID	CHROMOSPHERE	PERIGEE
MARS	ECLIPSE	COMET	JUPITER	MOON
EARTH	VENUS	PHOBOS	SUN	APHELION

61. One Famous Early Scientist Writes to Another

★ Below is the beginning of a letter from one famous person in the early scientific community to another. Complete the letter using as much knowledge about the two people as possible. You may continue on the back of this sheet, if necessary.

June 10, 1591

Dear Nicolaus Copernicus,

My name is Galileo. I would like to tell you about a strange invention called a telescope. I would also like to describe my ideas about our solar system.

_____

_____

_____

_____

_____

_____

_____

_____

_____

_____

_____

_____

_____

_____

Sincerely,

Galileo Galilei

62. Solar System Reverse Questions

★ Here is a reversal of sorts. You are given the answers to a series of questions regarding the solar system. Your task is to make an intelligent question that would be suitable for the answer.

1. Galileo made the discovery that the Milky Way was a series of stars and not just a band of light.

   _____

   _____

2. Centrifugal force throws a rotating object outward from a central location.

   _____

   _____

3. Planets follow elliptical or oval-shaped orbits.

   _____

   _____

4. Mars is the mysterious red planet.

   _____

   _____

5. The photosphere is the surface area of the sun.

   _____

   _____

6. Temperatures of sunspots are about 2000°F lower than the rest of the photosphere.

   _____

   _____

7. The four inner planets are Mercury, Venus, Earth, and Mars.

   _____

   _____

8. Jupiter is the largest planet in our solar system.

   _____

   _____

NAME _____   DATE _____

63. Solar System Connections

★   Nothing exists alone in the expanse of the universe; everything presently is
    or was part of something else. Your task is to tell in a complete sentence
    what the following list of things is
    or was part of. The first one has been
    completed for you.

Asteroids   _____Asteroids are part of the debris in space._____

Meteorite   _____

Earth   _____

Our Sun   _____

Jupiter   _____

Phobos   _____

Sunspots   _____

Chromosphere   _____

Our Moon   _____

Eclipse   _____

Atmosphere   _____

Comets   _____

Satellites   _____

64. One Famous Astronaut Writes to Another

★ Below is the beginning of a letter from one famous astronaut to another. Complete the letter using as much knowledge about the two people as possible. You may continue on the back of this sheet, if necessary.

February 20, 1962

Dear Neil Armstrong,

    My name is John Glenn. Today I am going to be the first American to orbit the Earth. This will help you to become _____

_____

_____

_____

_____

_____

_____

_____

_____

_____

_____

_____

_____

_____

_____

Sincerely,

John Glenn

"THAT'S ONE SMALL STEP FOR MAN, — ONE GIANT LEAP FOR MANKIND."

65. A Solar System Spiral

★ **Place the answers to the clues into the spiral puzzle grid in their number order. Be careful! Some answers will overlap.**

1. The largest planet in the solar system.

2. The name given to the east-to-west rotation of Venus.

3. The total or partial concealment of the sun by the moon.

4. The times of the year caused by the revolution of the Earth around the sun.

5. A dark area on the sun's surface.

6. The effect on Earth's oceans caused by the moon.

7. The red planet near Earth.

8. The name of the outer planet with large rings.

9. A bright object with a long flowing tail that has its own orbit.

10. The eighth planet from our sun.

11. The name of the solar wind interaction with the Earth's magnetic field.

12. The invisible line about which the Earth or any object rotates.

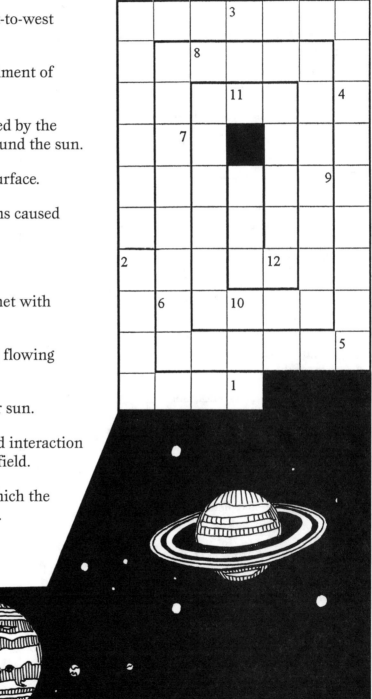

66. Moon Expressions from Clues and Scrambles

★ The descriptions in Column 1 are clues to finding the moon-related word or phrase you need for Column 3. Column 2 is the word or phrase you need for Column 3; however, it is scrambled. Place the unscrambled answer in Column 3.

Column 1—Clues	Column 2	Column 3
1. These mark the landscape of the lunar surface.	ATERCRS	_ _ _ _ _ _ _
2. This means "sea" in Latin.	AIMAR	_ _ _ _ _
3. This occurs when the moon crosses directly between the sun and the Earth.	CSPLEEI	_ _ _ _ _ _ _
4. Many of these have crashed into the moon's surface.	SEEITROTME	_ _ _ _ _ _ _ _ _
5. This is the period when the dark side of the moon faces the Earth.	EMONNWO	_ _ _ _ _ _ _
6. The name used when only a small part of the moon's lighted side can be seen from the Earth.	ESTCCNRE	_ _ _ _ _ _ _ _
7. The name used when half of the bright side of the moon is seen from Earth.	RTQURSTFIAER	_ _ _ _ _ _ _ _ _ _ _
8. The name of the moon phase after the first quarter.	BBIGOUS	_ _ _ _ _ _ _
9. The moon is called this in relation to the Earth.	TELSALETI	_ _ _ _ _ _ _ _
10. The moon does not possess this.	MSPEAREHOT	_ _ _ _ _ _ _ _ _ _
11. The moon's gravity is one-____ of the Earth's.	TXHSI	_ _ _ _ _
12. These are the remains of the moon's crust that were not covered by lava or debris.	GHANHILDS	_ _ _ _ _ _ _ _ _

67. The Solar System Wordsearch

★ Find and circle the answers in their correct locations across or down. The answers are scrambled after each clue.

G	A	L	A	X	Y	R	M	I	L	K	Y	W	A	Y	C	R	R	W	A
B	T	A	N	D	E	F	G	H	L	N	M	A	Y	U	M	I	L	P	L
H	P	H	O	T	O	S	P	H	E	R	E	N	J	E	R	W	T	R	P
Y	D	E	T	R	U	E	S	V	B	T	R	I	U	K	E	O	V	G	H
D	M	L	G	S	A	S	D	L	A	F	C	E	P	T	T	Y	E	N	A
R	I	I	R	U	T	Y	E	O	M	V	U	R	I	U	O	P	N	O	C
O	L	U	E	N	Y	G	A	P	N	I	R	P	T	P	O	N	U	P	E
G	J	M	T	S	H	P	R	I	I	P	Y	I	E	N	I	L	S	U	N
E	O	H	W	P	I	L	T	O	P	O	F	A	R	L	O	M	I	L	T
N	T	M	Q	O	M	I	H	P	O	S	B	S	M	N	I	B	M	N	A
E	U	A	U	T	F	V	E	T	C	O	M	E	T	S	C	A	O	P	U
R	W	R	A	S	X	W	A	S	L	S	P	G	M	A	B	D	P	R	R
B	E	S	F	W	A	S	T	E	R	O	I	D	S	D	R	E	I	M	I

1. A system or community of stars and planets. **(AAYXLG)**

2. A spiral galaxy. **(WAYYLIKM)**

3. Most of the mass of our sun is due to the gases **(ROGNEDHY)** and **(LIUMHE)**.

4. These are dark cooler areas on the sun's surface. **(USOSTPNS)**

5. Fragments of cosmic matter in space. **(STRODIEAS)**

6. Masses of cosmic dust and ice in their own orbit. **(OESTMC)**

7. Our nearest star, other than the sun. **(LACNREIHTAUPA)**

8. The source of Earth's warmth. **(NUS)**

9. The name of the surface of the sun. **(OTSHREPEPOH)**

10. The 4 inner plants. **(RTHAE) (ASRM) (URYCREM) (EUSNV)**

11. The largest plant in our Solar System. **(UPTIJER)**

68. Moon Data

★ Use the clues from the sentences to fill in the missing letters in the puzzle. The word you need is scrambled after each sentence.

The moon is not made up of this green, lactose-containing substance (1) . **HEESEC**

 (2) and (3) were the first persons to walk on the moon. **NDLARI, AMTONGRSR**

The moon has an effect on the (4) on earth. **SEITD**

The low, dark, flat areas of the moon are called (5) . **AAIMR**

Bright areas of the moon are called (6) . **NAHLGHIDS**

The moon is pockmarked with (7) . **SRARCTE**

 (8) vents are found in many low dark flat areas. **INLOVCAC**

Walled (9) seem to be the oldest moon features. **IALPNS**

Craters were probably caused by (10) hitting the lunar surface. **SROEMET**

When the Earth casts a shadow on the moon, this is called a (11) eclipse. **RNULA**

When the moon comes between the Earth and the sun, a (12) eclipse occurs. **RALSO**

#									
1.		H				E			
2.		L				N			
3.		R				O			
4.		I							
5.	M			A					
6.		I				N			
7.		R							
8.	V				N				
9.		L							
10.		E			S				
11.		U							
12.			L						

SECTION 4

Universe Concepts, Puzzles, and Ideas to Stimulate and Enrich

69. Universe Study: The Early Days

★ Find the word that should appear in each blank space. Write that word in the numbered spot at the left. A Choice Box has been provided.

1. _____
2. _____
3. _____
4. _____
5. _____
6. _____
7. _____
8. _____
9. _____
10. _____
11. _____
12. _____
13. _____
14. _____
15. _____
16. _____
17. _____
18. _____
19. _____
20. _____

QUICK ACCESS information

In the very early days of __1__, an ancient __2__ scientist named Pythagoras put forth the idea that the Earth was the __3__ center of the __4__. This was called the __5__ theory of the universe. This idea was not __6__ but it got others thinking.

In second-century Egypt, an astronomer named __7__ saw that __8__ seemed to be moving __9__ the Earth, but that the __10__ stood still.

In 1530, a Polish scientist named __11__ said that the planets moved around the __12__ in circles and not around the Earth.

Later on, in 1609, an Italian scientist named __13__ used a modification of a __14__ developed by Hans Lippershey to study the stars and planets. This invention or __15__ of the telescope dramatically __16__ scientists' __17__ of the universe.

When Galileo __18__ that the planets indeed did move around the sun, the idea was not taken seriously and was even __19__. Today, however, astronomers have come to know that the early work of Copernicus and Galileo was __20__ and worthy of respect.

CHOICE BOX

stationary	correct	ridiculed	astronomy	correct
Ptolemy	sun	geocentric	universe	around
Copernicus	Galileo	stars	study	telescope
Improvement	changed	planets	Greek	confirmed

70. Universe Adjectives

In our study of the universe, we look at many things, processes, and systems that can be better understood if we can describe aspects of each one.

★   Use <u>adjectives</u> to describe the following *things* of the universe.

(1) Galaxy	(2) Constellations	(3) Nebulae
(4) Milky Way	(5) Star	(6) Cepheids

★   Use <u>adjectives</u> to describe the following *processes* and *systems* of the universe.

(1) Astronomy	(2) Force	(3) Centrifugal Force
(4) Red Shift (Doppler Effect)	(5) Light Year	(6) Black Hole

71. Universe Study Search from Clues

★ The partially spelled Earth Science words, phrases, and terms below are related to or defined by the information or clue under each one. Your task is to complete the word, phrase, or term using the data or clues. A Choice Box has been provided.

1. _ _ I _ _ T_ _ _ _ _ _ _ S
   (*state of no weight*)

2. Z _ N _ _ _ _
   (*top of the celestial sphere*)

3. S_ _ _ _ T _ _ _ _
   (*a band of visible colors*)

4. M _ _ _ _ OR _ _ _
   (*space rock coming to Earth*)

5. S _ LAR _ _ _ _ _ _
   (*our sun is the center of this*)

6. _ AL _ _ _ _
   (*large group of stars*)

7. _ _ P _ _ _ _ EF _ _ _ _ _
   (*the Red Shift*)

8. _ _ _ _ _ T _ _ _ R
   (*distance light travels in one year*)

9. C _ N _ _ _ _ _ A _ _ _ _
   (*star pattern, such as Orion*)

10. _ _ A _ _ _ _ _
    (*attraction of matter*)

11. _ T _ _ _
    (*a sphere of gas that radiates heat and light*)

12. N _ B _ _ _
    (*dust and gas in interstellar space*)

13. B _ A _ _ _ _ OL _
    (*an object whose gravitational field absorbs light*)

14. _ _ T _ _ _ _ G _
    (*a false science using stars, etc.*)

15. _ _ G _ _ _ _ _ E
    (*classification of stars by brightness*)

16. _ _ V _
    (*a star that suddenly becomes brighter*)

17. S _ _ E _ _ _ _ _
    (*an object orbiting a parent body*)

18. _ _ _ _ _ A _
    (*a neutron star producing regular pulses of radiation*)

19. _ _ R _ _ _
    (*a distance of 3.26 light years*)

20. _ _ D _ REA _ _ _ _ _ _ _ D
    (*the time it takes a body to orbit a primary body*)

21. _ _ _ I _ T _ L _ _ _ _ _ E
    (*a tool used to observe with radio wavelengths*)

22. _ _ N
    (*a positively or negatively charged atom*)

23. _ OS _ _ _ _ _ _ _
    (*the study of the structure and development of the universe*)

24. _ _ _ _ _ _ Y S _ _ _ _ _
    (*a pair of stars orbiting a common center of gravity*)

25. _ _ _ _ _ _ _ MIC _ _
    U_ _T
    (*the average distance between the Earth and the sun*)

CHOICE BOX

WEIGHTLESSNESS	SPECTRUM	METEORITE	ZENITH	SOLAR SYSTEM
ASTRONOMICAL UNIT	GALAXY	DOPPLER EFFECT	GRAVITY	LIGHT YEAR
SIDEREAL PERIOD	BINARY STARS	CONSTELLATION	BLACK HOLE	SATELLITE
ASTROLOGY	PULSAR	PARSEC	COSMOLOGY	STAR
RADIO TELESCOPE	ION	MAGNITUDE	NEBULA	NOVA

72. Universe Newspaper Headlines

★ Here are two unusual newspaper headlines. Each one describes some sort of unusual situation. Your task is to write the rest of the newspaper story in the space provided. (You may continue on another sheet of paper, if necessary.) Include as many scientific details as possible.

RADIO TELESCOPE AIMED AT DISTANT GALAXY PICKS UP MUSIC

_____
_____
_____
_____
_____
_____
_____

ALL OF THE UNIVERSE, EXCEPT THE SUN AND EARTH, DISAPPEARS—SCIENTISTS NEED EXPLANATION

_____
_____
_____
_____
_____
_____
_____

73. Universe Tripod Connections

★   Listed below are 14 sets of three words that all have something in common
in the study of the universe. Identify what the words have in common and
write your answer in the space provided. A dictionary or glossary will help.

1.   star speed, star direction, spectrum   _____

2.   300,000 km/sec, light, 12 months   _____

3.   main sequence, giants, white dwarfs   _____

4.   Ursa Major, Ursa Minor, Cassiopeia   _____

5.   Kepler, Brahe, Newton   _____

6.   intense gravity, light capture, dense   _____

7.   clockwise, east to west, motion   _____

8.   Binary system, hydrogen gas, sudden brightness   _____

9.   Central Plane stars, cows, band of luminescence   _____

10.   space, matter, radiation   _____

11.   theory, Albert Einstein, space time continuum   _____

12.   3.26 Light Years, measurement, Earth orbit   _____

13.   path, revolve, gravitation   _____

14.   Aristotle, Ptolemy, Eratosthenes   _____

74. Deeper Universe Vocabulary with Missing Letters

★ The words below have every second pair of letters missing. Read the clue, then choose the correct missing pair of letters for each word from the Choice Box.

CLUES

1. ____ planets is the name of planets whose orbit is smaller than the Earth's.

IN		RI	

2. The name of the brightness radiated by a luminous object in space.

LU		NO		TY

3. Escape ____ is the speed needed to escape the gravitational field of a star.

	LO		TY

4. The measured amount of height from the surface of the Earth.

	TI		DE

5. ____ rays are produced by the explosion of a supernova.

	SM	

6. Mass per unit volume is used to compare mass of a celestial object to water.

	NS		Y

7. ____ stars have a common center of gravity they revolve around.

BI		RY

8. The movement of an object away from the observer.

RE		SS		N

CHOICE BOX

AL	IT	VE	OR	IC	MI
NA	SI	CO	DE	CI	TU
	CE		FE	IO	

75. Universe Speculation and Information

★ On line A, describe what you think the word or expression means.

★ On line B, give the dictionary or glossary definition of the word or expression.

1. Oblateness

(A) _____

(B) _____

2. Quasar

(A) _____

(B) _____

3. Main Sequence Star

(A) _____

(B) _____

4. Gravitation

(A) _____

(B) _____

5. Nebulae

(A) _____

(B) _____

6. Absolute Magnitude

(A) _____

(B) _____

7. White Dwarf

(A) _____

(B) _____

8. Red Giant

(A) _____

(B) _____

76. Universe and Solar System Expressions

★   Find the word or expression that does not belong to each group. Write that word in the space provided.

1. quasar, pulsar, sonar, nova   _____

2. Mars, Earth, Uranus, Phobos   _____

3. umbra, penumbra, eclipse, parsec   _____

4. altitude, height, depth, up   _____

5. asteroid, aphelion, meteor, rock   _____

6. photosphere, atmosphere, stratosphere,   _____
   ionosphere

7. astronomy, science, geology, astrology   _____

8. black hole, white hole, dense   _____

9. comet, Blitzen, dust, ice particles   _____

10. flare, sunspot, corona, Newton   _____

11. elastic, vernal equinox, autumnal equinox   _____

12. galaxy, universe, planet, Milky Way   _____

13. red giant, white dwarf, blue dwarf, main   _____
    sequence

14. fossil, satellite, orbit, revolution   _____

15. red shift, spectrum, Doppler, copper   _____

16. relativity, Einstein, theory, horses   _____

17. solar wind, prominence, thermal axis,   _____
    solar flare

18. star, planet, asteroid, carburetor   _____

19. Venus, Mercury, Earth, Saturn, Mars   _____

20. radiation, x-rays, highways, electromagnetic _____

77. Comets

★ Find the word that should appear in each numbered blank located in the paragraphs. Write that word in the numbered spot on the left. A Choice Box has been provided.

1. _____

2. _____

3. _____

4. _____

5. _____

6. _____

7. _____

8. _____

9. _____

10. _____

11. _____

12. _____

13. _____

14. _____

15. _____

16. _____

17. _____

18. _____

19. _____

20. _____

Comets are a 1 visible and unique feature of any 2 study. Comets 3 our attention because they become highly 4 as they approach a star like our 5 as they travel on their mostly 6 orbits.

Comets have three distinct 7 : the center or 8 , a nebulous cloud area called the 9 , and a long, highly visible 10 section that is actually 11 tails in one. The tail appears to flow 12 the comet because it is 13 that way by the solar 14 from the star it orbits.

Comets 15 in size as time goes on. This decrease in size is most 16 in the comets that 17 the sun most 18 because of the amount of matter lost at the point of 19 . This, along with the natural hazards of space travel, take their toll on comets. Because of these factors, comets with the 20 orbits are said to last the longest and be the most spectacular when they do return to the star or sun.

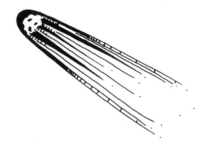

CHOICE BOX

elliptical	decrease	frequently	apparent	tail
sun	illuminated	wind	directed	coma
perihelion	grab	space	behind	nucleus
orbit	highly	largest	several	sections

NAME _____ DATE _____

78. Universe-Study Reverse Questions

★ Here is a reversal of sorts. You are given the answers to a series of questions regarding the study of the universe. Your task is to make an intelligent question that would be suitable for each answer.

1. The Orion Nebula is the brightest nebula visible from Earth.

_____

_____

2. The Milky Way is an example of a system of stars called a galaxy.

_____

_____

3. Astronomers look for radiant energy when they study the universe.

_____

_____

4. All bodies in the universe of space are moving.

_____

_____

5. The distance light travels in a year is called a light year.

_____

_____

6. Ursa Major and Ursa Minor are part of the star constellation containing the Big and Little Dippers.

_____

_____

7. A star's magnitude is the measure of its brightness.

_____

_____

8. The sun in our solar system is a yellow, main sequence star.

_____

_____

79. Space-Study Expressions

★ Study the descriptions of the universe and solar system terms. Then choose the correct answer from the Choice Box to fit each description.

1. The name of the celestial sphere immediately above an observer.

2. This is the darkest part of an eclipse cast by one stellar object onto another.

3. This is the point in time during a total solar eclipse when the sun cannot be seen at all.

4. The name given to the quick, huge, but temporary brightness of a star.

5. The name of a dark area appearing on the sun's photosphere.

6. The type of star that is the brightest and largest (for example, Antares).

7. The largest planet in our solar system.

8. A loose cluster of bright young stars.

9. The type of telescope used to observe electromagnetic radiation.

10. The name given to the time of the appearance of a visible area of an object in space (moon).

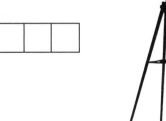

CHOICE BOX

| radio | supergiant | zenith | umbra | totality |
| Jupiter | supernova | open cluster | sunspot | phase |

80. Speedy Universe-Knowledge Puzzles

★ *Puzzle A*: Fill in the squares by unscrambling the letters above each grid. One universe-related word is vertical and one is horizontal.

A M S N U L E R B   U S L A Q R G A A X Y   A G E A N I I I T R V T Y

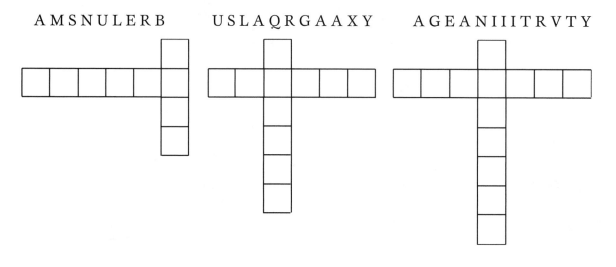

★ *Puzzle B*: Find five universe-related expressions in the following set of letters. All words read from left to right.

A B P U L S A R C D E S T A R F G M Q U N I V E R S E N O V A D E F M A G N I T U D E

_____ _____ _____ _____ _____

★ *Puzzle C*: Place the missing letters from the words in the corresponding locations on the grid to spell a universe-related word.

1	2	3	4	5	6	7	8	9

qu_1_sar   supe_4_nova   P_7_laris

pul_2_ar   s_5_lar   Ursa _8_ajor

s_3_ar   co_6_stellation   galax_9_

81. The Universe Wordsearch

★ Find and circle the answers in their correct locations across or down. The answers are scrambled after each clue.

P	A	R	S	E	C	M	B	E	L	T	Y	I	S	W	A	V	E	S	X
T	U	S	T	J	L	O	P	C	E	R	D	E	W	X	B	N	O	P	R
F	E	L	I	G	H	T	Y	E	A	R	U	M	P	W	R	O	M	Q	E
R	R	E	L	R	M	N	O	P	T	U	I	N	E	R	T	I	A	U	D
E	J	S	T	A	R	S	E	M	U	Q	R	E	W	I	P	T	G	E	S
Q	O	H	N	V	I	O	M	A	D	U	T	Y	V	W	K	F	N	V	H
U	S	O	G	I	A	N	T	S	E	A	L	P	P	G	N	A	I	T	I
E	N	T	S	T	M	I	K	S	T	S	O	T	U	M	I	O	T	I	F
N	H	E	R	Y	V	C	L	T	S	A	A	R	L	N	P	V	U	L	T
C	L	E	M	C	E	F	I	R	W	R	R	T	S	E	R	T	D	P	D
Y	I	N	E	B	U	L	A	E	A	B	U	C	A	M	O	L	E	O	M
E	F	K	L	E	R	M	B	V	E	R	T	Y	R	C	E	X	Z	L	U
C	O	N	S	T	E	L	L	A	T	I	O	N	S	I	O	L	R	T	Z

1. Unit of measure for interstellar space equal to 3.26 light years. **(ESRAPC)**
2. All forms of radiant energy travel in these. **(AESVW)**
3. The distance light travels in one year. **(GTLIH RAYE)**
4. Some groups of stars are known as this. **(COALLETSNSNIOT)**
5. Massive bright stars. **(ANTSIG)**
6. A large body of rarefied gas and dust in interstellar space. **(BUALEN)**
7. Spheres of gas that give off light. **(RASTS)**
8. The tendency of an object to remain still if still, or, if moving, to go on moving in the same direction unless acted upon by an outside force. **(IETAINR)**
9. The number of waves per second. **(RQECYNUEF)**
10. This is also known as the Doppler Effect. **(DIFTRESH)**
11. The mutual attraction of matter. **(RVTYIAG)**
12. The classification of stars by brightness. **(ANIDUTGME)**
13. Its name stands for quasi stellar radio source. **(USRAQA)**
14. The measure of the quantity of matter often in a body like a star. **(SSMA)**
15. These are sources of radio sounds that pulse at a regular rate. **(USRSALP)**

SECTION 5

CHEMISTRY: FUNDAMENTAL SKILL BUILDERS

82. Chemistry Vocabulary

★ Search each puzzle grid for four chemistry words that are *related* to the particular heading. (The words are found across and down.) After you circle the words on the puzzle grid, write them on the lines below the heading.

H	Y	D	R	O	G	E	N	D
Y	D	F	U	P	L	O	R	E
S	U	L	P	H	U	R	I	C
O	R	D	E	L	K	R	I	N
U	D	E	R	K	R	E	T	S
R	E	F	G	H	I	L	M	R

ACID

_____

_____

_____

_____

C	A	T	A	L	Y	S	T	M
L	A	T	Y	S	T	E	B	K
E	R	C	A	L	T	A	O	O
P	R	O	L	B	E	M	N	L
C	O	M	P	O	U	N	D	S
M	O	P	G	H	I	L	S	M
E	N	E	R	G	Y	E	R	N

CHEMICAL REACTIONS

_____

_____

_____

_____

HYDROGEN

T	A	S	T	E	L	E	S	S
A	R	R	C	E	N	W	E	D
M	O	D	O	R	L	E	S	S
D	E	W	M	N	O	P	R	O
R	E	W	M	N	I	K	L	M
C	O	L	O	R	L	E	S	S
W	R	E	N	L	P	R	O	D

_____

_____

_____

_____

83. Basic Chemical Processes and Substance Expressions from Clues and Scrambles

★ The descriptions in Column 1 are clues to finding the chemical process or substance word you need for Column 3. Column 2 is the word you need for Column 3; however, it is scrambled. Place the unscrambled answer in Column 3.

Column 1—Clues	Column 2	Column 3
1. You do this to test a hypothesis.	XEIEETNMRP	_ _ _ _ _ _ _ _ _ _
2. This is a substance consisting of two or more kinds of atoms that have joined.	OUMCPOND	_ _ _ _ _ _ _ _
3. The name of the process of changing from a gas to a liquid.	IOOENNCSATDN	_ _ _ _ _ _ _ _ _ _ _ _
4. This is the name given to the splitting of the nuclei of certain types of atoms.	SIOFNSI	_ _ _ _ _ _ _
5. This is the name given to the joining of the nuclei of certain types of atoms.	UONSFI	_ _ _ _ _ _
6. This is the process by which a substance takes up another substance into itself.	ASPTINROBO	_ _ _ _ _ _ _ _ _ _
7. The basic chemical structure of petroleum is called this.	YDCANOBRHRO	_ _ _ _ _ _ _ _ _ _ _
8. The name of the central part of an atom that possesses protons and neutrons.	LUSNUCE	_ _ _ _ _ _ _
9. This is two or more atoms joined together.	LOMCULEE	_ _ _ _ _ _ _ _
10. This is an explanation about the knowledge of a process of nature.	OHTREY	_ _ _ _ _ _
11. This is a mixture that is homogenous and transparent or clear.	UTLSOION	_ _ _ _ _ _ _ _
12. This is a murky, heterogenous mixture with identifiable particles.	UPNOISESSN	_ _ _ _ _ _ _ _ _ _

84. What's the Matter, Atom?

★ On line A, describe what you think the word or expression means.

★ On line B, give the dictionary or glossary definition of the word or expression.

1. Atom (A) _____
   (B) _____

2. Molecule (A) _____
   (B) _____

3. Base (A) _____
   (B) _____

4. Compound (A) _____
   (B) _____

5. Mixture (A) _____
   (B) _____

6. Solution (A) _____
   (B) _____

7. Weight (A) _____
   (B) _____

8. Mass (A) _____
   (B) _____

85. Chemical Elements and Symbols

★ The clues are the symbols of 15 chemical elements. Your task is to locate the correct name of each element in the grid. The answers can be found across and down. One is done for you.

CLUES

C

N

Fe

Cu

H

O

He

Ne

Zn

Ni

Ca

Ag

Pb

Hg

Au

P	C	A	R	B	O	N	T	R	Y	P	E	R	M
O	K	E	C	A	L	I	R	O	N	C	E	F	H
M	E	D	I	U	V	T	N	E	R	G	L	O	P
D	C	O	P	P	E	R	J	H	R	E	U	P	D
E	R	T	R	W	A	O	X	Y	G	E	N	T	S
W	A	S	B	E	R	G	E	D	R	E	T	V	M
A	Z	U	I	H	E	E	C	R	A	L	C	I	R
N	I	T	N	E	O	N	E	O	M	E	R	T	V
R	O	E	G	L	J	U	T	G	C	A	T	E	R
B	I	T	N	I	D	G	H	E	F	E	R	I	C
V	W	E	R	U	F	Z	I	N	C	D	E	R	M
C	A	L	N	M	E	R	Z	I	T	R	J	O	H
J	O	N	H	T	E	C	F	C	N	S	W	A	T
E	R	B	C	A	R	A	M	K	S	O	N	K	A
E	T	Y	N	S	I	L	V	E	R	T	H	Y	K
J	P	L	E	R	F	C	D	L	R	I	S	A	T
E	P	I	L	T	R	I	E	A	N	T	Y	O	N
M	I	M	E	R	C	U	R	Y	N	A	L	A	S
C	R	U	A	S	T	M	U	E	G	E	N	S	T
G	O	L	D	B	D	R	I	D	E	E	G	V	W

86. Matter and Atom "Not the Same As" Vocabulary

★ Read each sentence starter below. Each one states that a particular matter and atom topic is not the same as another. Your task is to explain how they are different.

1. Gravity is not the same as grams because _____
   _____

2. Matter is not the same as vacuum because _____
   _____

3. Nucleus is not the same as orbit because _____
   _____

4. Protons are not the same as neutrons because _____
   _____

5. Element is not the same as atom because _____
   _____

6. Atomic number is not the same as mass number because _____
   _____

7. Periodic table is not the same as isotope because _____
   _____

8. Molecule is not the same as compound because _____
   _____

9. Acid is not the same as base because _____
   _____

10. A salt is not the same as an oxide because _____
    _____

87. Grouping Chemistry Expressions

★ Choose two words or expressions from the Choice Box that *relate* to each "target" word or expression. Cross off the words after you use them. No word can be used more than once. Some words may not be used at all.

"Target" Word/Expression	Related Words and Expressions
1. Density	
2. Chemical Bonds	
3. Chemical Reaction	
4. Physical Change	
5. Fermentation	
6. Base	
7. Acid	
8. Alloy	
9. Atom	
10. Catalyst	

CHOICE BOX

specific gravity, change in shape, attraction, release energy, change in size, mix of metals, sugar to alcohol, better use of metals, adhesive force, smallest to exist, neutralizes acid, remains unchanged, bacteria, contains hydrogen, chemical change, less than 7 pH, mass, has properties of element, speeds reactions, alkali

88. Chemical Expressions

★   Below are a number of important chemical science definitions. Place the correct expression in front of the definition, then find that expression in the puzzle. All answers are vertical as well as horizontal within the same answer. (The first one has been done for you.) A Choice Box has been provided.

1.   __Physical change__   is the change in size, shape, or state of matter.

2.   _____ is a property that determines how an element or compound will react with different elements or compounds.

3.   _____ is a property that can be identified as not being or causing a chemical reaction in a substance.

4.   _____ is the force that holds atoms together.

5.   _____ is the change in the chemical makeup or composition of matter.

6.   _____ is the name we use when we compare the density of a substance to the density of water.

7.   _____ is another name for definition 5.

E	R	E	L	A	T	I	V	E	P	H	Y	C	H	E	M	I	C	A	L
C	H	E	M	I	C	A	L	D	S	I	C	H	E	M	I	C	A	L	C
L	E	M	P	R	O	M	B	E	C	A	L	R	A	C	T	I	O	P	H
A	C	H	E	M	R	P	O	N	S	P	H	Y	S	I	C	A	L	R	A
T	P	R	O	L	M	N	N	S	C	H	E	M	I	C	A	L	P	O	N
I	C	E	M	I	C	A	D	I	P	R	C	A	T	O	M	R	R	P	G
P	H	Y	S	I	C	A	L	T	M	E	R	T	I	O	N	E	O	E	E
V	M	A	T	Y	R	T	C	Y	B	R	A	K	W	C	H	A	P	R	M
E	C	H	E	M	O	P	H	C	H	W	E	M	B	O	D	C	E	T	N
C	D	F	R	E	T	D	A	P	R	O	L	M	K	L	W	T	R	Y	O
H	W	E	R	S	U	I	N	C	H	J	K	L	O	P	O	I	T	R	I
Y	B	R	U	S	Y	C	G	P	Y	S	I	C	R	S	E	O	Y	O	N
M	T	U	S	T	R	I	E	P	R	O	L	I	N	S	T	N	C	P	R

CHOICE BOX

chemical bond	chemical reaction	~~physical change~~	chemical property
relative density	chemical change	physical property	

89. The A"Maze"ing Atom

★ Follow the trail of correct answers in the maze below to reach the end of the puzzle. Watch out for false "rabbit" trails. The first one is done to help you get started.

1. _____ is anything that takes up space and has mass.
   (THINGS, MATTER, MONEY)

2. A(n) _____ is the smallest unit of an element.
   (MOLECULE, ATOM, ADAM)

3. The central part of an atom is the _____.
   (NOSE, SMACK DAB, NUCLEUS)

4. _____ and _____ are two kinds of particles found in the nucleus.
   (PROTONS, RONRONS, NEUTRONS, ATOMRONS)

5. _____ move around the nucleus of an atom.
   (IONS, ELECTRONS, BOOTRONS, AROUNDTRONS)

6. The path of an electron is its _____. **(ORBIT, HABIT, DISCONTINUITY)**

7. The _____ properties of protons, electrons, and neutrons dictate how they will act. **(ELECTRICAL, EMOTIONAL, CHEMICAL)**

8. Protons have a(n) _____ charge. **(NEGATIVE, POSITIVE, IMPERATIVE)**

9. Electrons have a _____ charge. **(QUICK, NEGATIVE, SERVICE)**

10. Neutrons have _____ charge. **(NO, NEGATIVE, PAY PER VIEW)**

Start
↓

M	T	B	S	W	E	R	A	S	T	Y	E	L	E	C	G	H	P	R	O
O	A	E	R	T	Z	E	S	K	I	L	O	P	R	E	W	S	E	O	M
N	M	T	T	E	R	A	T	O	M	N	M	U	C	W	U	E	R	T	N
E	B	E	R	T	A	C	A	T	E	O	U	X	R	E	P	R	T	O	R
Y	W	R	E	N	D	A	M	N	W	S	A	C	L	C	E	S	N	S	E
E	L	R	W	F	U	I	P	L	C	E	T	H	R	E	N	B	E	R	T
N	O	R	T	C	E	L	E	S	N	O	R	T	U	M	J	U	I	T	E
S	W	B	I	T	E	L	E	C	T	R	I	C	A	L	P	O	S	I	T
O	R	Y	O	W	R	T	E	C	V	P	R	E	M	G	E	N	E	V	I
M	A	Y	N	A	T	R	E	D	M	R	E	D	A	T	I	V	E	N	O

↑
Finish

90. Quick, Learn the Chemical Element

★   Listed below are 15 chemical elements and 15 symbols of chemical elements. Place each symbol beside its correct element. Then locate each element in the grid with its symbol immediately following it. The first one is done for you.

B	S	H	Y	H	C	A	R	B	O	N	C	J	U	Z	G	C	B	N	O
U	I	C	H	Y	O	P	L	M	C	W	E	R	T	I	A	O	S	J	X
T	L	O	E	D	G	O	L	D	A	U	V	E	R	N	S	P	O	U	Y
L	V	W	L	R	H	L	P	M	I	C	W	E	R	C	W	P	D	D	G
E	E	I	I	T	R	A	D	I	U	M	R	A	B	Z	V	E	I	F	E
W	R	L	U	O	F	E	R	R	I	N	W	Z	E	N	O	R	U	E	N
B	A	V	M	N	T	P	O	I	N	C	P	I	R	W	N	C	M	R	O
M	G	E	H	W	N	W	E	R	I	R	O	N	F	E	T	U	N	T	Y
A	T	Y	E	M	N	R	P	O	T	I	C	R	T	Y	M	E	A	Y	P
V	N	I	C	K	E	L	N	I	S	I	L	I	C	O	N	S	I	C	O
S	U	L	F	U	R	S	T	F	G	H	Y	J	U	P	L	N	E	M	N
U	L	M	E	T	B	Y	P	O	W	E	S	T	W	T	Y	U	M	Z	I
M	E	R	C	U	R	Y	H	G	H	Y	D	R	O	G	E	N	H	R	A

ELEMENT

Gold	Au
Silver	____
Iron	____
Hydrogen	____
Copper	____
Carbon	____
Mercury	____
Helium	____
Zinc	____
Silicon	____
Sulfur	____
Radium	____
Oxygen	____
Nickel	____
Sodium	____

SYMBOL

Cu
Hg
Ag
He
~~Au~~
Si
Ra
Ni
H
O
Na
Fe
S
C
Zn

C

Au

Zn

S

91. The Chemical Symbol Wordsearch

★ Search the puzzle to find the chemical symbols for the selected elements listed below. Place each symbol beside its element as you find it in the puzzle. Each symbol begins with an uppercase letter and ends with a lowercase letter. Where there is no second letter in the chemical symbol, only the uppercase is used. Circle the answers in the wordsearch. The first one is done for you.

E	A	P	b	G	J	A	M	o	X	Z	L	i	A	E	G	L	M	G	A
A	D	G	L	T	Q	X	(A	l)	y	x	a	Z	A	E	F	Q	R	N	e
R	a	T	K	Z	A	D	E	G	L	P	t	Z	J	L	Z	M	A	E	G
Z	E	D	L	E	M	S	b	T	R	T	V	Z	S	Y	A	u	D	N	i
D	G	L	T	R	n	M	Q	T	V	A	r	Z	T	A	D	G	J	L	N
B	r	Q	L	M	Y	T	S	n	Z	A	Y	D	R	E	G	J	T	V	n
W	X	T	i	T	Y	G	D	B	M	U	T	P	u	A	L	M	H	e	T
T	Z	T	J	C	d	j	N	a	Q	E	M	T	T	Q	O	Z	T	A	H
M	g	g	j	n	E	D	L	D	K	r	T	C	l	Z	G	L	P	T	Z
L	B	T	V	Z	Y	A	M	n	Z	D	T	E	A	g	T	I	T	F	e
S	i	Z	C	a	Z	T	D	E	X	H	g	R	T	Z	A	A	Z	A	Z
A	E	V	Z	D	A	M	C	r	M	Z	Z	Z	A	C	o	D	A	D	T
E	s	M	Q	T	Z	Y	T	Q	Z	n	D	C	T	M	E	Z	L	C	u

Aluminum __Al__   Einsteinium ____   Manganese ____   Radium ____

Antimony ____   Fluorine ____   Mercury ____   Radon ____

Argon ____   Gold ____   Molybdenum ____   Silicon ____

Boron ____   Helium ____   Neon ____   Silver ____

Bromine ____   Hydrogen ____   Nickel ____   Sodium ____

Cadmium ____   Iodine ____   Nitrogen ____   Sulfur ____

Calcium ____   Iron ____   Oxygen ____   Tin ____

Carbon ____   Krypton ____   Phosphorus ____   Titanium ____

Chlorine ____   Lead ____   Platinum ____   Tungsten ____

Chromium ____   Lithium ____   Plutonium ____   Uranium ____

Cobalt ____   Magnesium ____   Potassium ____   Zinc ____

Copper ____

SECTION 6

PHYSICAL SCIENCE CONCEPTS FOR THE MODERN CLASSROOM

92. Physical States of Matter

★ Read the paragraph below and unscramble the letters in each blank to form the word necessary to complete the meaning of the sentence. Write the word correctly in the numbered space to the left.

QUICK ACCESS
information

1. _____
2. _____
3. _____
4. _____
5. _____
6. _____
7. _____
8. _____
9. _____
10. _____
11. _____
12. _____
13. _____
14. _____
15. _____
16. _____
17. _____
18. _____
19. _____
20. _____

At any given time and under the right set of (1) IRUSECNATSCCM, all (2) BSECNATSSU can exist in one of the physical states of matter. These states of matter or phases are known as (3) OIDLS, (4) IUDIQL, and (5) SAG. A (6) HSEAP is known as an observable part or portion of matter. If we (7) BSEREOV a solid, we see that it has a high degree of (8) CEINOSHO. The (9) LESELUCOM or (10) OMSTA have a strong attracting (11) ECRFO on each other. This results in a (12) DESNE, compact solid with a definite (13) HPAES. The molecules and atoms of liquids, on the other hand, have a (14) SSEREL degree of cohesion than solids but still tend to (15) MANIRE together. The atoms and molecules in a (16) QUIDIL are not tightly bound and (17) EVOM much more freely than in a solid, which accounts for their ability to (18) APSHE themselves to the form of any container. The atoms and molecules in a gas have only (19) NLAMIIM cohesion and move almost freely. Under normal circumstances, a gas will occupy all of the area of its (20) RNTINEAOC. The gas container must be sealed or the gas will escape.

93. Standardization of Power

★ Unscramble the letters in each row and place them in the grid. Then put each answer with its corresponding number in the paragraph below to reveal a fact about standardized power measurement.

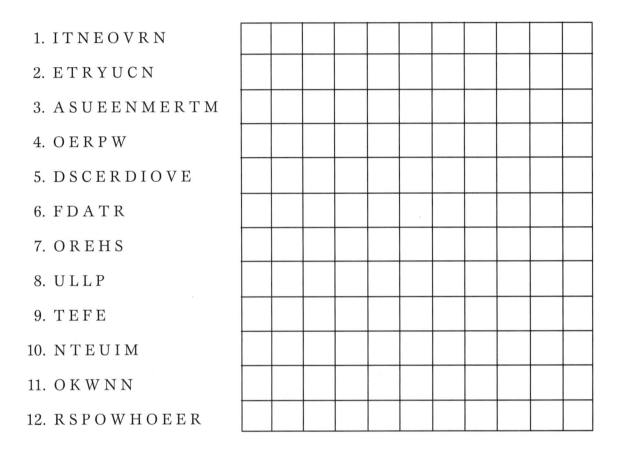

1. I T N E O V R N

2. E T R Y U C N

3. A S U E E N M E R T M

4. O E R P W

5. D S C E R D I O V E

6. F D A T R

7. O R E H S

8. U L L P

9. T E F E

10. N T E U I M

11. O K W N N

12. R S P O W H O E E R

James Watt, a Scottish (1) _____ in the 18th (2) _____, standardized the (3) _____ of (4) _____. He (5) _____ that one strong (6) _____ work (7) _____ could (8) _____ 165 pounds 200 (9) _____ in one (10) _____. This became (11) _____ as one (12) _____. The formula was standardized to:

$$1 \text{ hp} = \frac{165 \text{ lb.} \times 200 \text{ ft.}}{1 \text{ min.}}$$

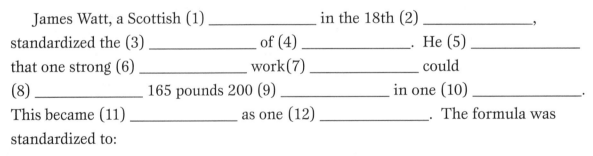

94. Double-Sided Antonyms
for Relative Conditions of Matter

★ Listed below are 17 relative conditions of or influences upon matter. You are to find their opposites. The words to be found in Puzzle A have antonyms (word opposites or near opposites) in Puzzle B. The words and their antonyms begin at the same place in each puzzle, but some words have longer or shorter antonyms.

★ Circle the word in either Puzzle A or B and then circle its antonym in the other puzzle.

★ Write the correct antonyms next to the words listed below. Some are found in Puzzle A and some are found in Puzzle B. One is done for you to help you get started.

Puzzle A

V	A	R	I	A	B	L	E	B	C	A	W	C
D	E	N	S	E	L	O	A	M	I	D	E	O
U	S	E	F	U	L	P	B	O	C	F	A	N
H	G	D	U	L	L	C	S	T	F	M	K	D
A	C	I	L	M	B	A	O	I	D	N	O	E
B	E	D	D	A	R	K	L	O	M	W	I	N
V	A	C	U	U	M	U	U	N	X	P	V	S
E	C	X	W	Q	T	C	T	Z	A	T	D	A
S	A	T	U	R	A	T	E	D	D	A	J	T
L	A	R	G	E	K	O	P	I	C	W	H	I
T	C	I	O	P	M	H	E	A	V	Y	M	O
T	R	A	N	S	P	A	R	E	N	T	J	N
O	L	D	J	A	P	H	O	T	U	D	R	Y

Puzzle B

C	O	N	S	T	A	N	T	D	E	F	S	E
S	P	A	R	S	E	I	R	S	R	E	T	V
U	S	E	L	E	S	S	E	T	B	E	R	A
L	P	S	H	I	N	Y	L	I	M	L	O	P
P	O	S	B	T	I	X	A	L	I	E	N	O
X	S	B	L	I	G	H	T	L	E	R	G	R
F	I	L	L	E	D	K	I	N	A	B	C	A
B	E	R	L	F	V	E	V	E	F	H	G	T
E	M	P	T	Y	R	O	E	S	X	N	Z	I
S	M	A	L	L	P	N	A	S	N	P	J	O
C	T	E	R	L	I	L	I	G	H	T	I	N
O	P	A	Q	U	E	U	L	R	E	S	T	U
N	E	W	E	L	T	C	O	L	D	W	E	T

1. variable   __constant__
2. evaporation   _____
3. wet   _____
4. hot   _____
5. weak   _____
6. dense   _____
7. heavy   _____
8. useful   _____
9. filled   _____

10. opaque   _____
11. relative   _____
12. saturated   _____
13. motion   _____
14. dark   _____
15. dull   _____
16. old   _____
17. large   _____

95. Five Processes that Change the State of Matter

★   Read each sentence starter below. Each one states that one process is not the same as another. Your task is to explain how these processes are different. Be sure to use complete, proper sentences.

1. Melting is not the same as freezing because _____

_____

2. Melting is not the same as evaporation because _____

_____

3. Freezing is not the same as evaporation because _____

_____

4. Freezing is not the same as condensation because _____

_____

5. Evaporation is not the same as sublimation because _____

_____

6. Melting is not the same as sublimation because _____

_____

7. Freezing is not the same as sublimation because _____

_____

8. Condensation is not the same as evaporation because _____

_____

9. Condensation is not the same as melting because _____

_____

10. Sublimation is not the same as condensation because _____

_____

96. A Physical Properties Puzzler

★ Below are ten descriptions of the physical properties of matter. Study the words in the Choice Box and choose the correct word to fit each description. Place your answers in the answer boxes.

1. The total amount of matter in an object

2. The compact hard form of a substance

3. The vapor form of a substance

4. The outward contour of an object

5. Occupied space expressed in cubic measure

6. The force that gravity exerts on a body

7. The appearance of an object due to its hue

8. The ratio of the mass of an object to its volume

9. The ability of an object to be pressed or hammered into shapes without being broken

10. The fluid form of a substance

CHOICE BOX

density	solid	liquid	volume	weight
color	mass	shape	gas	malleability

97. What Do You Know About Energy?

★ Use the clues from the sentence to fill in the missing letters in the puzzle grid. The word you need is scrambled after each sentence.

1. Energy stored in _____ is used in most transportation. **LEUFS**

2. Energy is defined as the ability to do _____. **ORKW**

3. Food going into your _____ will release energy. **OYBD**

4. Substances like fuel and food have _____ energy stored in them. **LIMHCECA**

5. The energy form called hydroelectricity is produced by moving _____. **AERTW**

6. Old Faithful in Yellowstone National Park gives off _____ energy. **ERMALHTOGE**

7. _____ energy comes from the sun. **LSORA**

8. _____ energy is generated at nuclear power plants. **LRIEECTCAL**

9. _____ energy sources are not destroyed while being used. **BLEAWEREN**

10. _____ energy sources are destroyed while being used. **BLEAWENRNENO**

Copyright © 2003 by John Wiley & Sons, Inc.

1.	F	U		L					
2.	W		R						
3.		O	D						
4.	C		E			A			
5.	W		T		R				
6.	G		O		H		R		A	L
7.	S		L						
8.	E			C					L
9.	R		N		W	A		L	E
10.		O		R		N		W		L	E

98. Particle Theory of Matter

★ Listed below are the basic concepts describing the particle theory of matter; however, some key words have been left out. Search for those words in the Choice Box and fill in the blanks. Then circle the words in the puzzle grid.

A	C	V	E	R	T	V	C	D	C	E	F	Q	U	T	R	I	M	K	M
P	T	M	I	N	D	S	T	R	O	N	G	E	R	L	O	P	E	S	O
L	D	A	N	I	P	T	A	S	N	V	G	H	T	I	K	A	R	D	V
A	T	T	R	A	C	T	E	D	T	E	W	R	T	C	A	M	C	E	E
S	F	T	T	R	I	C	T	E	I	D	E	N	T	I	C	A	L	S	M
P	O	E	A	E	R	T	Y	E	N	O	P	K	I	M	O	P	O	M	E
E	P	R	T	A	W	W	E	R	U	L	P	O	N	J	N	I	S	N	N
R	J	W	D	E	A	C	L	E	O	G	H	T	Y	O	S	L	E	T	T
T	O	E	R	R	I	L	M	A	U	K	A	Z	V	P	I	J	R	O	P
S	T	M	A	S	P	A	C	E	S	M	A	L	L	Q	S	K	E	B	I
U	R	K	M	G	H	R	G	B	I	J	O	N	U	T	L	C	R	R
V	W	E	I	T	Y	G	P	U	R	H	K	R	T	I	S	A	M	E	T
W	A	R	E	T	Y	E	T	A	N	O	T	H	E	R	R	P	I	D	E

1. All _____ in the universe _____ or is made up of
   _____ or _____ particles.

2. All small or tiny particles of the _____ material are
   _____.

3. The tiny particles are _____ to one _____. The
   attraction gets _____ as the particles get _____
   together.

4. The particles are not so _____ as the _____ between
   them.

5. The tiny particles are in _____ _____.

CHOICE BOX

tiny	stronger	same	large	another
identical	closer	continuous	small	movement
spaces	consists	attracted	matter	

99. Matter: Eliminating the Negative and Explaining "Why"

★ This assignment is unusual because you are *not* to choose the correct answer to fit into the space in each sentence. Instead, *you must choose (circle) the least correct answer*. There are three possible answers at the end of each sentence. One is absolutely correct or true, one could be true, and one is false or completely wrong. You must explain *why* the answer you circled is completely wrong or incorrect, or how it does not fit the context of the sentence.

1. ____ is said to be anything that occupies space and has mass.
   (Vacuum, Matter, Thing)

   _____
   _____

2. ____ is defined as the opposition or resistance to motion or movement.
   (Friction, Force, Direction)

   _____
   _____

3. A(n) ____ is the smallest part of an element.   **(atom, particle, theory)**

   _____
   _____

4. Protons have a ____ charge.   **(negative, positive, plus)**

   _____
   _____

5. Chemical ____ contain more than one element.
   (intelligence, compounds, combinations)

   _____
   _____

6. ____ are the smallest parts of a compound.   **(Microns, Molecules, Fossils)**

   _____
   _____

7. ____ are the result of the physical combining of different materials.
   (Substances, Fixtures, Mixtures)

   _____
   _____

100. Physical Science Newspaper Headlines: Part One

★ Here are three unusual newspaper headlines. Each one describes some sort of unusual situation. Your task is to write the rest of the newspaper story in the space provided. (You may continue on another sheet of paper, if necessary.) Include as many scientific details as possible, so each one may require physical science research.

STUDENT DESCRIBES "LAW OF THE PENDULUM"— WINS GRANDFATHER CLOCK

_____

_____

_____

_____

_____

_____

GRAVITY GETS STRONGER, THINGS ARE HEAVIER— BRILLIANT STUDENT EXPLAINS

_____

_____

_____

_____

_____

_____

STUDENT GIVES WONDERFUL ARGUMENT WHY U.S. SHOULD GO METRIC

_____

_____

_____

_____

_____

_____

101. Physical Science Newspaper Headlines: Part Two

★ Here are three unusual newspaper headlines. Each one describes some sort of unusual situation. Your task is to write the rest of the newspaper story in the space provided. (You may continue on another sheet of paper, if necessary.) Remember to use proper punctuation and spelling. Each one may require physical science research.

STUDENT GOES BACK IN TIME—INTERVIEWS ALBERT EINSTEIN

_____
_____
_____
_____
_____
_____

STUDENT COMPARES MASS AND WEIGHT—
FEELS ASSIGNMENT IS "HEAVY"

_____
_____
_____
_____
_____
_____

STUDENT FINDS DENSITY CAN BE USED TO IDENTIFY
SUBSTANCE UNDER DESK—TELLS HOW

_____
_____
_____
_____
_____
_____

102. "Heated" Vocabulary

★ Choose the heat-related words from the Choice Box to complete the spelling of the words in this grid. Not all words in the Choice Box will be used.

				G			O	T	H		R	M		L			
								H									
					S			H	E		T						
								M									
							S	O		A							
							C	O		D							
			M		T		M	P	E		A	T		R	E		
								L									
C		O	L			F	R		E	Z				P			
		T				R											
														N			
			N			Z	E		O		C	L		I		S	
						E						I					
				E	N	E		G								L	
												N					
																D	

Choice Box

gas	thermograph	freeze	hot	geothermal	expansion
volume	energy	temperature	zero	cool	Celsius
cold	lukewarm	contraction	frozen	joule	heat
solid	solar	thermocouple	melting		

115

103. Turn Up the Heat

★ Locate the answers to the heat puzzle clues in the grid boxes A, B, or C. Answers can be vertical and horizontal within the same answer. A Choice Box has been provided. The numbers above each box indicate which question's answers are in that box. Question 12 has been answered for you to help you get started.

A: 2, 9, 10, (12), 13

T	H	E	R	M
T	H	E	R	O
C	E	V	M	C
O	X	O	O	O
N	P	L	G	U
T	A	U	R	P
R	N	M	A	L
A	S	E	P	E
C	I	T	H	V
T	O	N	X	P
I	O	N	E	I

B: 1, 3, 4, 8, 11

C	G	A	L	I
E	C	N	B	L
L	L	I	T	E
S	I	A	Y	O
I	N	F	S	T
U	I	R	M	O
S	C	O	X	C
T	A	Z	N	T
H	L	E	M	T
E	B	N	I	A
R	M	O	S	T

C: 5, 6, 7, 14, 15

H	E	A	T	M
T	M	J	O	E
I	P	H	V	L
B	V	C	O	T
P	I	O	M	I
E	P	L	R	N
V	S	D	B	G
A	D	I	C	E
P	W	S	N	T
O	X	D	O	X
R	A	T	I	S

1. In science, most temperature measurements are in this scale.

2. Air goes through ___ when heated.

3. ___ invented the first thermometer.

4. A ___ regulates temperature in a room or appliance.

5. ___ is energy that is moved from a hotter entity to a colder entity.

6. ___ is the change of a substance (ice) from one state to another (water).

7. ___ is the lack of heat or warmth.

8. The name for the solid state of ice.

9. The ___ of matter can change depending on the amount of heat.

10. Air goes through ___ when cooled.

11. A ___ thermometer measures body temperature.

12. ___ is a thermometer that needs electricity to measure temperature.

13. ___ uses infrared light to make a photographic measure of temperature.

14. ___ is the change of a substance (water) from one state to another (water vapor).

15. This is the name of frozen H_2O.

CHOICE BOX

expansion	thermostat	contraction	Galileo	clinical
thermocouple	thermograph	heat	cold	volume
ice	evaporation	frozen	melting	Celsius

104. Powerful Forces

★   Study the descriptions of the forces-related terms. Then choose the correct
     answer from the Choice Box to fit each description.

1. This force resists the movement
   of an object as it touches another.

2. This force is the pull or attraction
   one body has on another.

3. This force is produced by moving
   two surfaces against each other.

4. This is a force that moves away
   from a center point.

5. The upward force of a liquid.

6. The force that either pulls or
   pushes in a field around a
   magnet.

7. The force that needs to be
   overcome in order to make a
   machine work.

8. The resistance to change unless
   acted upon by outside force.

9. The force applied to a body.

10. This is the electric force in any
    form of electrical energy.

CHOICE BOX

stress	inertia	buoyancy	electromotive	gravity
friction	magnetism	electrostatic	centrifugal	load

QUICK ACCESS information

105. The Difference Between Mass, Volume, and Weight

★ Find the word from the Choice Box that should appear in each numbered blank located in the following paragraphs. Write the words in their corresponding numbered blank on the left. No word may be used more than once.

1. _____

2. _____

3. _____

4. _____

5. _____

6. _____

7. _____

8. _____

9. _____

10. _____

11. _____

12. _____

13. _____

14. _____

15. _____

16. _____

17. _____

18. _____

19. _____

20. _____

The term "mass" refers to the amount of substance or _1_ in an _2_.

The term "volume" refers to the actual _3_ of the object. The size can change but the _4_ will remain _5_. For example, when water in a cup freezes, it _6_, increasing the volume, but the amount of water or mass stays the _7_.

Weight is _8_ from mass and _9_ because the weight of an object is the amount of _10_ pull on an object. It differs from mass in that _11_ will change from one _12_ to the next but mass will not change. Let's look at an astronaut. While the person is in the _13_ suit walking to the space shuttle on Earth before takeoff, he/she may have an _14_ weight of 270 pounds. (This is why an astronaut walks slowly to the shuttle.) Fifteen minutes after _15_ off, astronauts weigh zero pounds because they are in space and have _16_ the _17_ of the _18_ gravity. They can _19_ around in what on Earth was a 270-lb. weight. The mass of the person and the mass of the space suit have not _20_, only their weight has changed.

CHOICE BOX

mass	weight	accumulated	material	size
blast	float	Earth's	escaped	different
expands	gravitational	constant	force	space
same	location	volume	changed	object

106. The Mechanical Advantage of a Lever

QUICK ACCESS
information

Mechanical advantage of our lever

calculated as $\dfrac{\text{Effort arm}}{\text{Resistance arm}} = \dfrac{8}{2} = 4$

★   Fill in the blanks with answers from the Choice Box.

Mechanical advantage is the (1) _____ of the load or the amount of (2) _____ to the (3) _____ or effort it takes to overcome it. The amount of aid we (4) _____ from the use of a machine is its mechanical advantage. The lever is a (5) _____ that, while it (6) _____ you to increase force, it does (7) _____ save work. The distance from the (8) _____ to the point of (9) _____ force is the effort arm. The (10) _____ from the fulcrum to the weight is the resistance arm. As you (11) _____ force downward at point (12) _____, you will move the weight at point A (13) _____.

When you move C all the way down, you will find that point C has moved (14) _____ than the weight at point (15) _____. The distance the force (16) _____ is greater than the distance the (17) _____ moves. What you achieve by (18) _____ force, you lose in the distance the weight moves. This makes the work (19) _____. What you put in is what you get out, only in (20) _____ forms.

CHOICE BOX

A	resistance	not	distance	ratio
C	increasing	machine	different	apply
weight	farther	force	fulcrum	equal
enables	moves	upward	receive	downward

107. What Does That Tool Do?

★ Below is a list of common everyday machines and tools we all use. Describe the main function of the tool or machine. Then list the secondary or other functions of the tool or machine. The main function is worth 10 points. Each secondary function is worth 5 points. Write your total number of points at the bottom of this page. Good luck!

Tool or Machine	Main Function	Secondary or Other Function
Shovel		
Wheelbarrow		
Leash		
Hammer		
Saw		
Power drill		
Blender		
Tweezers		
Pen		
Axe		
Fly swatter		
Pry bar		

Total Points:

_____

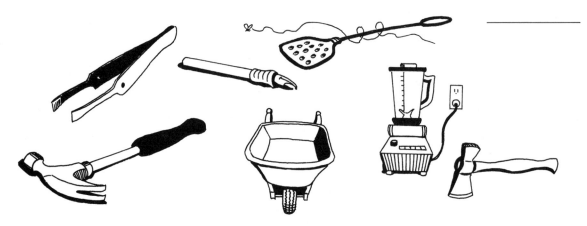

108. Sound "Not the Same As" Vocabulary

★ Read each sentence starter below. Each one states that one sound-related thing is not the same as another. Your task is to explain how they are different.

1. Sound wave is not the same as water wave because _____

   _____

2. Compression is not the same as rarefaction because _____

   _____

3. Transmitted is not the same as echo because _____

   _____

4. Absorbed is not the same as reflected because _____

   _____

5. Decibel is not the same as energy because _____

   _____

6. Amplitude is not the same as noise because _____

   _____

7. Sonar is not the same as radar because _____

   _____

8. Mach number is not the same as ultrasonic because _____

   _____

9. Vibration is not the same as wave length because _____

   _____

10. Frequency is not the same as pitch because _____

   _____

109. It Sounds to Be True

★ Here is a list of clues. Each clue describes a word associated with sound. The answer for each clue is one of two scrambled words at the end of each sentence. Unscramble each set of words to get the correct answer for each clue and write it on the line.

1. Sound travels in the form of _____.
   SVEWA   ODG

2. Sound may be _____ or passed through matter other than air. **AESNRTMITTD   ESRHO**

3. Sound that is trapped is said to be _____.
   ODSL   DBROSABE

4. Sound that comes back to the source is said to be _____.
   DECEFERLT   TSOL

5. The number of sound waves that passes a location in a given period of time is said to be its _____. **LECAP   RUNYCEEFQ**

6. The distance from the crest of one sound wave to the crest of the next sound wave is called its _____. **STTHNERG   GEEAWVLNTH**

7. How high or low a sound seems to be is called its _____.
   IDTHC   ICTPH

8. The area of crowded air particles in a sound wave is called _____.
   EMCOPRSSION   DPOR

9. Sound vibrations per second are measured in _____. **ZEHRT   SIAV**

10. The degree of loudness of a sound wave depends on the amount of _____ in it. **STNAHPELE   EYGREN**

11. Sounds that are not pleasing to hear are called _____.
    SYOB   ESINO

12. When an airplane travels faster than the speed of sound, it is said to be _____. **ISEUSPRONC   TSAF**

13. The amount of energy in a sound wave is known as its _____.
    EDUTAMPLI   NSEVE

14. The loudness of a sound is measured in _____.
    SLICDEBE   WREPO

15. A high frequency sound used to locate objects underwater is called _____. **NILO   ANSOR**

Copyright © 2003 by John Wiley & Sons, Inc.

NAME _____   DATE _____

110. Light "Not the Same As" Vocabulary

★ **Read each sentence starter below. Each one states that one light-related thing is not the same as another. Your task is to explain how they are different.**

1. <u>Absorbed</u> is not the same as <u>reflected</u> because _____

_____

2. <u>Mirror</u> is not the same as <u>glass</u> because _____

_____

3. <u>Infrared waves</u> are not the same as <u>ultraviolet waves</u> because _____

_____

4. A <u>vacuum</u> is not the same as <u>atmosphere</u> because _____

_____

5. <u>Transmitted</u> is not the same as <u>received</u> because _____

_____

6. <u>Transparent</u> is not the same as <u>translucent</u> because _____

_____

7. <u>Clear</u> is not the same as <u>opaque</u> because _____

_____

8. A <u>prism</u> is not the same as a <u>spectrum</u> because _____

_____

9. <u>Frequency</u> is not the same as <u>hertz</u> because _____

_____

10. <u>Concave</u> is not the same as <u>convex</u> because _____

_____

111. Physical Science Vocabulary Vowelless Puzzle

★ Listed in the Choice Box are some of the most important words associated with Physical Science. Your task is to find the correct Physical Science words in the puzzle. All of the vowels (A, E, I, O, U, Y) have been removed. You will need to write the vowels in place as you find the words.

CHOICE BOX

LIGHT	ADHESION	MOLECULE	WORK	KINETIC
VELOCITY	CALORIE	CONDUCTOR	FRICTION	MASS
VISCOSITY	CELSIUS	DENSITY	INERTIA	WEIGHT
WAVE	ATOM	ENERGY	ION	GRAVITY

112. How One Thing Is Like Another in Physical Science

★ Many things in Physical Science have similarities, even though at first they may appear to be very different. Your task is to describe how the first item (A) is somehow like the second item (B). Be sure to use complete, proper sentences for your answers.

1. (A)   Energy   (B) Work

_____

_____

2. (A)   Adhesion   (B) Cohesion

_____

_____

3. (A)   Alternating Current   (B) Direct Current

_____

_____

4. (A)   Amplitude Modulation   (B) Frequency Modulation

_____

_____

5. (A)   Gravity   (B) Magnetism

_____

_____

6. (A)   Momentum   (B) Centrifugal Force

_____

_____

7. (A)   Friction   (B) Inertia

_____

_____

8. (A)   Atom   (B) Molecule

_____

_____

ENERGY   WORK

113. Physical Science Tripod Connections

★   Listed below are 14 sets of three words that all have something in common in the study of Physical Science. Identify what they have in common and write your answer in the space provided. A dictionary or glossary will help.

1.   vapor   evaporation   oxygen   _____

2.   thermodynamics   thermocouple   thermometer   _____

3.   watt   volt   ohm   _____

4.   stress   strain   statics   _____

5.   ultrasonic   sonic   wave   _____

6.   proton   neutron   electron   _____

7.   kilogram   meter   kiloliter   _____

8.   galvanometer   ohmmeter   speedometer   _____

9.   attraction   electromagnet   iron   _____

10. waves   decibels   flute   _____

11. infrared   ultraviolet   electromagnetic _____

12. luminescence   fluorescence   laser   _____

13. mirror   concave   convex   _____

14. acceleration   velocity   momentum   _____

COOL   2 COOL   3 COOL

NAME _____ DATE _____

114. Physical Science Problem-Solving with Brainstorming

★ Your class will get into groups of not more than 5 members each. Each student is to use this sheet. You are to discuss the central problem and come up with the most workable solution. Here are the brainstorming rules:

- There are no wrong responses.
- No one is allowed to criticize someone else's response.
- Try to arrive at the most workable answer to the problem.
- Use responses from yourself and others to get better solutions.
- There are 12 possible responses to help solve the problem. Write them below.

Problem: **The world is losing heat (thermal energy) at an alarming rate.**

1. _____
2. _____
3. _____
4. _____
5. _____
6. _____
7. _____
8. _____
9. _____
10. _____
11. _____
12. _____

Most workable solution: _____

Problem: **Aliens have come demanding supplies of four forms of energy. They appear threatening.**

1. _____
2. _____
3. _____
4. _____
5. _____
6. _____
7. _____
8. _____
9. _____
10. _____
11. _____
12. _____

Most workable solution: _____

115. Unusual Physical Science (Physics) Problems

★ Listed below are six unusual situations that somehow relate to physical science (physics). Give the most scientific explanation possible for what is occurring in each statement **or** explain scientifically what you would do in each situation. Use the back of this sheet if you need more space for your answers.

1. You can shoot thermal energy from the tip of your index finger.

   _____

   _____

2. You are skydiving but not falling. Everyone else opens his or her chute, but you are stuck in the air.

   _____

   _____

3. You discover on your way to school that you now have the ability to make things levitate or float in the air.

   _____

   _____

4. You arrive home from school with modern physics ideas in your brain and immediately you are thrust back to the year 1440.

   _____

   _____

5. You accidentally fall in front of a speeding bus, but you are not hurt or marked. The bus merely bounces off your chest and now has a big dent where it hit you.

   _____

   _____

6. Your tennis serve is so powerful that the ball explodes as it smashes right through the webbing. Your opponents are worried.

   _____

   _____

NAME _____   DATE _____

116. Physical Science Search from Clues

★ The partially spelled Physical Science words, phrases, and terms below are related to or defined by the information or clue under each one. Your task is to complete the word, phrase, or term using the data or clues. A Choice Box has been provided.

1. __ __ __ __ __ Y
(*the ability to do work*)

2. __ L __ __ __
(*a substance that flows*)

3. __ __ __ V __ __ __
(*attraction between two things [planets]*)

4. __ __ ICT __ __ __
(*resistance on the surface of two things*)

5. __ __ __ T
(*a form of energy*)

6. __ N __ __ __ __ A
(*the resistance of a body to acceleration or deceleration*)

7. K __ L __ __ __
(*the degree of temperature in the absolute scale*)

8. __ __ H __ S __ __ __
(*the binding of the atoms of two different materials*)

9. __ __ S __ R __ __ __ __ __
(*the taking up of energy*)

10. __ __ P __ I __ __ __ __
__ODUL __ __ __ __ __
(*A.M.*)

11. __H __ __ __ AL   E __ __ __G__
(*energy consumed or released by chemical reaction*)

12. __RO__NI__ __   M__ __ION
(*random movements of particles in liquid or gas*)

13. __ F __ __ __ __ __ __ __ __ __
(*the ratio of energy input to output*)

14. __ __ __ ECU __ __
(*the smallest identifiable part of a substance*)

15. __ __ __ I __ __ __ __
(*the force gravity has on a body*)

16. S__ __F__ __ __ __   T__ __ __ I__ __
(*elastic action of a liquid surface*)

17. __ __ __ __ S   __UM__ __ __
(*the total protons and neutrons in an atom*)

18. __ __ CH __ __ __ __ __ __
(*the study of the action of force on matter*)

19. D __ N __ __ __ __ __
(*the study of bodies in motion*)

20. AB __ __ __ __ __ __ __   Z __ __ __
(*the lowest temperature possible*)

21. __ __ R __ __ __ __
(*the force applied on a body*)

22. __ __ __ __ __ CI __ __ __
(*the rate a body moves in a direction*)

23. __ O __ D
(*the force to be overcome to do work*)

24. __ __ __ S
(*the amount of matter in a body*)

25. __ __PI__LA__ __   __C__ __ __ __
(*movement up or down caused by surface tension of a liquid*)

CHOICE BOX

BROWNIAN MOTION	EFFICIENCY	INERTIA	ABSORPTION	GRAVITY
AMPLITUDE MODULATION	VELOCITY	MASS	FRICTION	MASS NUMBER
SURFACE TENSION	LOAD	STRESS	MECHANICS	FLUID
ABSOLUTE ZERO	ENERGY	HEAT	MOLECULE	ADHESION
CAPILLARY ACTION	WEIGHT	KELVIN	DYNAMICS	CHEMICAL ENERGY

117. Physical Science Words and Expressions

★ Place the answers to the following Physical Science statements or clues in the spaces provided. Answers are scrambled at the end of the sentences.

1. The path radiant energy travels is called a _____. **(AYR)**

2. The resistance of a body to acceleration or deceleration is called _____. **(TEINRTA)**

3. An atom that has either gained or lost one or more electrons is called a(n) _____. **(NOI)**

4. The study of motion alone is called _____. **(TAMNKIEICS)**

5. The determining of motion of an object acted upon by forces is known as _____. **(SCINDYAM)**

6. The study of the flow of fluids is called _____. **(LRIDAHYUCS)**

7. Devices that transmit energy are called _____. **(EHAMCINS)**

8. The _____ is the simplest of machines. **(RVLEE)**

9. A set of wheels used to increase the power applied to a resistance is called a _____. **(YLLPUE)**

10. When an object or set of objects is in balance, it is said to be in _____. **(UIRLIUEQIBM)**

11. The study of the behavior of objects held stationary by forces is called _____. **(IASTTCS)**

12. The rate of doing work is _____. **(RWOPE)**

13. The flow of heat through solids is called _____. **(OIDNCOUCT)**

14. The degree of disorder in a system is _____. **(RTENOPY)**

15. The rate at which a body moves in a particular direction is called _____. **(ILVEOCTY)**

Copyright © 2003 by John Wiley & Sons, Inc.

118. Double-Sided Physical Science Synonyms

★ Listed below are 18 words related to physical science. You are to find their synonyms (words that mean the same). The words to be found in Puzzle A have synonyms in Puzzle B. The words and their synonyms begin at the same place in each puzzle, but some words have longer or shorter synonyms.

★ Circle the word in either Puzzle A or B and then circle its synonym in the other puzzle.

★ Write the correct synonyms next to the words listed below. Some are found in Puzzle A and some are found in Puzzle B. One is done for you to help you get started.

Puzzle A

M	P	A	R	T	B	R	O	M	W	S	C	K
A	R	F	A	T	O	M	I	C	A	U	O	I
T	O	O	E	X	C	E	L	A	O	B	M	N
T	D	R	F	U	S	E	D	M	R	S	P	E
E	W	C	R	I	D	W	R	O	E	T	A	T
R	M	E	A	D	E	L	E	L	S	I	R	I
F	C	O	N	V	E	R	T	E	P	T	A	C
I	G	N	I	T	E	N	J	C	O	U	T	D
D	F	I	S	S	I	O	N	U	N	T	I	O
E	N	E	R	G	Y	C	R	L	S	I	V	E
M	A	I	N	T	A	I	N	E	E	O	E	W
T	H	E	R	M	A	L	R	E	D	N	M	K
D	R	U	W	R	I	N	C	R	E	A	S	E

Puzzle B

S	C	O	M	P	O	N	E	N	T	E	R	M
U	R	P	N	U	C	L	E	A	R	X	E	O
B	A	O	S	U	R	P	A	S	S	C	L	T
S	T	W	J	O	I	N	E	P	R	H	A	I
T	W	E	D	E	R	M	W	A	E	A	T	O
A	D	R	L	M	O	P	C	R	A	N	I	N
N	C	H	A	N	G	E	A	T	C	G	V	O
C	O	M	B	U	S	T	R	I	T	E	E	P
E	S	P	L	I	T	R	A	C	I	L	V	M
W	O	R	K	R	S	Y	O	L	O	M	O	Y
C	O	N	S	E	R	V	E	E	N	E	R	T
H	E	A	T	R	E	T	E	M	K	A	R	E
R	A	T	G	H	G	A	I	N	K	I	L	R

1. energy _____

2. kinetic _____

3. component _____

4. thermal _____

5. force _____

6. relative _____

7. excel _____

8. exchange _____

9. convert _____

10. combust _____

11. reaction _____

12. fission _____

13. fuse _____

14. conserve _____

15. matter   substance

16. gain _____

17. nuclear _____

18. molecule _____

119. A Properties of Matter Puzzler

★ Many materials are chosen for various purposes because of certain features they possess, which are called properties. Read the description of each property. Then choose the correct answer from the Choice Box and fill in each grid.

1. Resistance to this property prevents squishing a material.

2. This type of stress on a material will pull it apart.

3. The ability to resist stress is said to give the material this.

4. The price of a material controls this.

5. The beauty of a material will control this.

6. Aromatic cedar is often chosen for building because of this property.

7. You can compare the strengths of many materials by how they respond to this.

8. The situation that occurs when a material becomes weak from overuse or wrong use is called this.

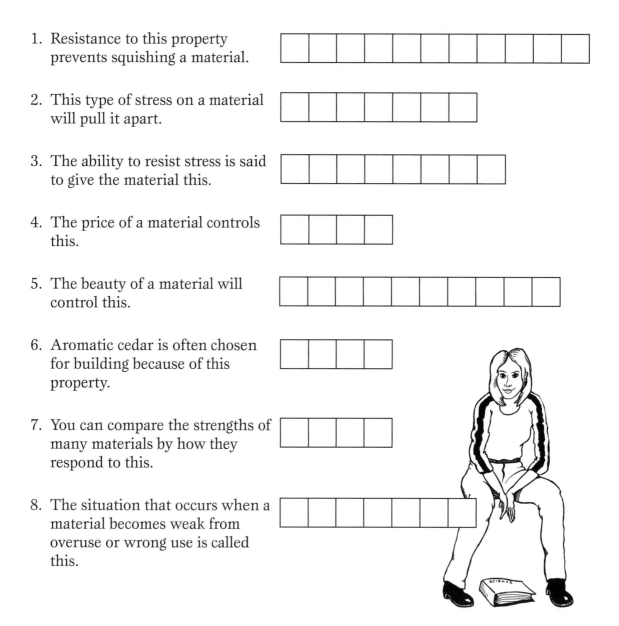

CHOICE BOX

tension	strength	odor	compression
appearance	load	fatigue	cost

120. Energy, Work, and Power

★ Use all the letter pairs in the Choice Box to fill in the answers to the clues about energy, work, and power.

__1__ is another name for speed.

__2__ energy is heat energy.

__3__ energy can exist without matter.

__4__ energy is moving waves of pressure.

__5__ is non loss of energy.

__6__ energy does not have a solar source.

Energy is the ability to do __7__ .

__8__ is energy in motion.

Molecules move faster when the __9__ is higher.

__10__ energy is the result of a chemical reaction.

Energy can neither be __11__ nor __12__ .

1.	VE		CI			
2.		ER		L		
3.		DI		T		
4.	SO		D			
5.	CO	NS			ON	
6.		CL		R		
7.		RK				
8.	KI			C		
9.	TE		ER		UR	E
10.	CH		IC			
11.	CR			D		
12.		ST	RO		D	

CHOICE BOX

TI	AL	TI	MA	AN	ER
RA	NE	LO	NU	EM	AT
EA	TH	EA	UN	TY	YE
DE	TE	WO	MP	VA	

121. Mr. Newton and His Laws of Motion

QUICK ACCESS
information

★ From the Choice Box below, find the word that should appear in each numbered blank located in the paragraphs. Write the word in the correct numbered blank on the left. No word may be used more than once.

1. _____
2. _____
3. _____
4. _____
5. _____
6. _____
7. _____
8. _____
9. _____
10. _____
11. _____
12. _____
13. _____
14. _____
15. _____
16. _____
17. _____
18. _____
19. _____
20. _____

There are three basic laws that describe the _1_ of an object acted upon by outside forces. These were _2_ by a true _3_: Isaac Newton (1664–1727).

_4_ first law of motion tells us that an _5_ will remain at _6_, or an object will remain in motion unless it is _7_ upon or influenced by some sort of force. For example, a ball _8_ in the middle of a field needs the _9_ of a student to get it going, or the ball needs the hands of the student to _10_ it as it flies through the air. The student is the _11_ force.

Newton's _12_ law describes how an object (ball) will behave when a force acts _13_ it. This law states that the amount or _14_ of change of _15_ of an object equals the force placed upon it. This brings us to the related idea of _16_, which is the tendency for a body to _17_ change in its state of rest or motion (in a straight line).

Newton's _18_ law of motion looks at the natural association between forces produced by objects. It tells us that if one object exerts a force on a second object, this second object will exert an _19_ and _20_ force on the first. This is called the principle of action and reaction.

A BODY AT REST.. ..TENDS TO STAY AT REST.

CHOICE BOX

outside	kick	third	resist	inertia
object	equal	acted	rate	sitting
Newton's	momentum	rest	upon	genius
stop	second	motion	developed	opposite

122. Friction Grids

★ Locate the answers to the friction puzzle clues in the grid boxes A or B. Answers can be vertical and horizontal. A Choice Box has been provided. The numbers above each box indicate which question's answers are in that box.

A: 1, 2, 6, 7, 10, 11, 13, 15

R	E	D	T	B	A	M	T	A
E	S	D	E	R	E	S	B	T
S	N	O	L	U	M	W	E	M
I	B	R	A	K	E	T	R	O
S	T	O	P	P	I	N	G	S
T	P	U	R	O	U	B	E	P
A	L	G	E	A	G	I	N	H
N	N	H	E	L	E	J	E	E
C	A	R	R	I	E	S	R	R
E	O	H	N	S	T	O	A	E
W	A	T	A	N	H	Y	T	B
T	E	B	R	E	G	M	E	R
A	N	C	A	F	O	R	C	E

B: 3, 4, 5, 8, 9, 12, 14

J	O	I	N	T	S	A	L	L
C	A	T	R	E	J	O	U	I
N	T	S	O	N	E	H	B	Q
T	I	E	A	C	A	R	R	U
R	A	L	R	B	W	E	I	I
E	N	C	A	R	T	I	C	D
S	D	R	N	V	C	L	A	S
K	G	A	O	A	R	E	N	X
H	E	L	T	H	E	A	T	W
T	R	A	O	T	A	W	R	E
A	O	J	E	G	E	G	F	A
W	G	Q	U	I	C	K	E	R
A	S	T	N	O	K	S	R	I

1. Friction is a ___ that inhibits or resists motion.
2. When you measure friction, you measure the amount of this.
3. This is a sign of friction.
4. The higher the friction, the ___ the wear.
5. Friction can also act in this, such as water.
6. Friction is necessary for ___ a car.
7. The friction you ___ while swimming allows you to go forward.
8. Friction affects the ___ of the human body.

9. Friction affects ___ things on Earth.
10. When surfaces are uneven or ___, friction is increased.
11. The wear on the ___ pedal of a used car can be an indicator of wear on the car.
12. Oil in a motor is a ___ used to reduce friction.
13. When the space shuttle returns, it must deal with friction as it enters Earth's ___.
14. Friction can cause this.
15. Wind can help create friction as it ___ sand and other particles against objects.

CHOICE BOX

resistance	quicker	force	heat	liquids
brake	stopping	lubricant	generate	joints
atmosphere	carries	all	rough	wear

SECTION 7

HOOKED ON LIFE SCIENCE TECHNIQUES, IDEAS, AND CONCEPTS

123. A Cell Puzzler

★ Using only the letters given below, find the words that complete the statements. Some letters are used more than once.

L	O	N	H
G	T	M	S
P	V	I	U
E	A	C	R
B	W	Y	D

1. _____ is a team of cells that performs a special function.

2. The _____ is the control center of a cell.

3. _____ are tiny units that control most cell activities.

4. _____ are threadlike structures in the nucleus of cells that contain genes.

5. _____ contain stored food for cells or waste material from cells.

6. _____ are bundles of chlorophyll in plant cells.

7. _____ is the process of cell division.

8. A cell _____ is the living part that surrounds a cell and helps control the movement of matter into and out of plant and animal cells.

9. The cell _____ is the thick nonliving barrier in plant cells.

10. _____ is the jellylike material that surrounds the nucleus of cells.

124. Match the Cells

★ **Place the numbers from the definitions next to the correct word for each definition.**

1. The living barrier around a cell.

2. The nonliving barrier around plant cells.

3. These contain food for the cell or waste materials of the cell.

4. The jellylike material surrounding an animal nucleus. It has many small structures that keep the cell alive.

5. Threadlike units in the nucleus of animals cells.

6. They are on the chromosomes of animal cells, and they control most of the cell's activities.

7. What scientists call multi-celled living things.

8. Chloroplasts contain bundles of this in most plant cells.

9. This is the process whereby cells reproduce by cell division.

10. This surrounds the nucleus of animal cells.

_____ chromosomes

_____ organism

_____ cell wall

_____ vacuoles

_____ chlorophyll

_____ mitosis

_____ genes

_____ cell membrane

_____ nuclear membrane

_____ cytoplasm

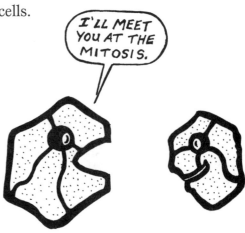

125. Animal and Plant Cell Differences and Similarities

★ Animal cells and plant cells have both different cell structures and similar cell structures. Look at the diagrams and label each with the correct components from the list in the middle. The A and P indicate if the structure is found in the animal cell, the plant cell, or both.

ANIMAL CELL   **PLANT CELL**

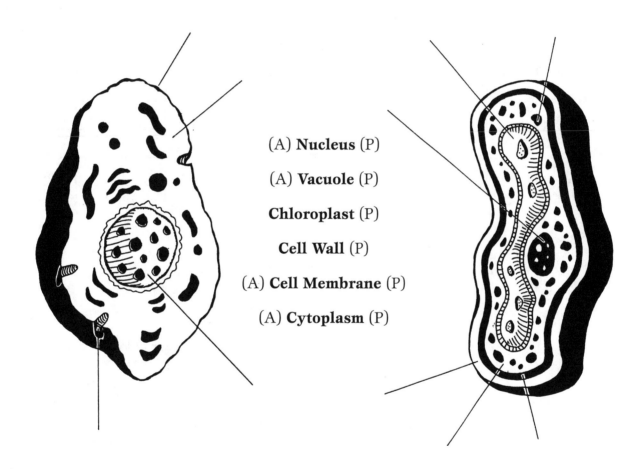

(A) **Nucleus** (P)

(A) **Vacuole** (P)

Chloroplast (P)

Cell Wall (P)

(A) **Cell Membrane** (P)

(A) **Cytoplasm** (P)

126. Unscramble the Living Matter Words

★ Locate and circle the answers to the living matter clues in the grid. The answers have been provided after the clues; however, they are scrambled. Study the clue, then decipher the answer.

P	C	Y	T	O	P	L	A	S	M	T	N	U	C	L	E	U	S	X	C
B	O	R	N	E	C	T	R	I	V	E	R	W	U	T	R	A	Q	U	E
P	R	C	H	L	O	R	O	P	L	A	S	T	J	U	P	I	R	M	L
R	W	G	I	D	F	G	H	I	K	L	E	R	T	P	U	I	I	M	L
O	A	E	D	C	H	L	O	R	O	P	H	Y	L	L	P	R	B	O	M
T	S	N	E	M	I	P	R	E	R	D	G	J	M	A	L	N	O	V	E
E	T	E	R	D	R	I	G	V	E	W	I	H	T	S	K	O	S	I	M
I	O	S	S	F	E	D	A	P	F	A	T	S	D	T	E	L	O	L	B
N	J	V	T	N	D	E	N	W	E	T	C	R	E	I	R	E	M	A	R
S	O	C	U	R	O	S	D	E	R	E	W	Q	U	D	T	W	E	R	A
H	T	I	S	S	U	E	C	H	A	R	E	W	A	S	Y	I	S	T	N
N	O	S	T	N	W	A	Y	R	E	T	Y	S	E	R	T	N	U	I	E
C	A	R	B	O	H	Y	D	R	A	T	E	S	Y	S	T	E	M	M	R

ACROSS

1. The thick liquid substance in cells. **(YCLSMATOP)**

2. These are energy providers containing carbon, hydrogen, and oxygen. **(ABODYHCRRASET)**

3. The control center of a cell. **(SECNULU)**

4. The place where the plant cell's manufacturing processes are carried on. **(TRHCLOPSOAL)**

5. This allows a plant to make its own food. **(LRHCLOMPOYL)**

6. Groups of similar cells with a similar job. **(ESSTIU)**

7. When a group of organs work correctly together, they are called this. **(ESYSTM)**

8. These are compounds for energy storage. **(ATFS)**

DOWN

9. These are large complex organic compounds of amino acids. **(RETOPSNI)**

10. The outer boundary of a cell. **(BMLECLEMRENA)**

11. These are the instructions and directions for making the completed products of the cell. **(SEEGN)**

12. These are formations or structures in the cell that make proteins from amino acids. **(EOOIRBSMS)**

13. These give flowers their color. **(SISLPATD)**

14. A group of different tissues working together to do a job, e.g., heart. **(GROAN)**

15. A basic necessity for life. **(EAWTR)**

127. What Is It? Knowing Reproductive Processes from Clues

★ Use the clues from the sentences to fill in the missing letters in the puzzle.
The answers are at the end of each sentence, but they are scrambled.

1. Reproduction is the process by which _____ things make their own kind. **(VILING)**

2. _____ is the name of reproduction by dividing into two new cells. **(ISIFSON)**

3. _____ is the name of a female reproductive cell. **(GGE)**

4. _____ is the name of the male reproductive cell. **(PRMES)**

5. As the male sperm and female egg unite, they form a cell called a _____. **(YOZETG)**

6. The process of the male sperm joining with the female egg is called _____. **(NOIERTAFZILIT)**

7. In the early stages of fertilized development, an organism is called an _____. **(MROEYB)**

8. Traits or features that a parent passes to a child are called _____ traits. **(HTIREINED)**

9. A _____ gene is the one that determines the trait in an individual even when other genes are present. **(OMTDNANI)**

10. A _____ gene for a trait remains hidden if the dominant gene for that trait is also present. **(ESSERECIV)**

1.	L					G		
2.		I					N	
3.			G					
4.	S			M				
5.			G					
6.	F			I				... N
7.			B					
8.			H					
9.	D				A			
10.			C				E	

128. Grouping Life Science Vocabulary

★ Choose three words or expressions from the Choice Box that fit or are associated with each Life Science topic. Cross off the words after you use them. No word can be used more than once. Some words may not be used at all.

Life Science Topic	Words
1. Amphibians	
2. Biomes	
3. Birds	
4. Cell	
5. Climate	
6. Environment Responses	
7. Fish	
8. Hibernation	
9. Insects	
10. Primates	
11. Protective Coloration	
12. Reptiles	
13. Rodents	
14. Teeth	
15. Tree	

CHOICE BOX

salamander	grasshopper	rain	genes	slow body activity	nucleus
bark	rat	grassland	molars	surrounding conditions	mouse
adaptation	sparrow	trout	tundra	gorilla	storms
iguana	newt	baboon	salmon	biological clock	butterfly
gibbon	disguise	oak	incisors	canines	crow
hawk	stored fat	ant	alligator	growth rings	carp
sleep	crocodile	region	camouflage	deciduous forest	vacuoles
area	weather	mimicry	squirrel	phototropism	frog

Copyright © 2003 by John Wiley & Sons, Inc.

129. Life Science Vocabulary Relationships

★ Below are two lists of Life Science vocabulary words or phrases. Match the word or phrase on the left with the word or phrase on the right that is *related* to it by placing the appropriate number in the space provided. Then locate the given word or phrase in the left-side puzzle, and locate its related word in the right-side puzzle. One has been done for you.

Left Side

E	N	V	I	R	O	N	M	E	N	T	B	B	X	L
O	P	N	I	M	U	B	A	W	P	R	O	T	N	I
B	A	C	T	E	R	I	A	I	P	E	N	O	M	G
N	O	P	I	C	D	A	S	W	M	E	S	V	A	H
A	Q	U	S	X	T	R	U	W	R	S	T	I	U	T
M	U	T	S	A	R	W	D	W	X	C	T	R	A	R
R	T	Y	U	A	I	K	L	O	P	M	R	U	S	E
S	D	A	E	T	R	A	P	M	I	T	O	S	I	S
M	A	S	J	H	K	L	M	O	P	N	R	T	A	P
C	O	N	T	R	O	L	C	E	N	T	E	R	I	O
E	A	R	L	Y	O	R	G	A	N	I	S	M	O	N
Y	A	R	T	R	V	B	R	P	I	L	O	E	V	S
C	H	L	O	R	O	P	L	A	S	T	I	P	L	E

Right Side

C	E	L	L	D	I	V	I	S	I	O	N	D	E	R
P	H	O	T	O	T	R	O	P	I	S	M	I	P	E
N	F	K	L	O	P	E	R	W	T	F	U	S	K	D
U	M	B	L	P	E	R	T	R	U	C	S	E	E	F
C	H	L	O	R	O	P	H	Y	L	L	C	A	R	G
L	O	P	T	O	M	K	L	O	P	E	L	S	M	H
E	A	T	D	T	E	N	R	T	R	E	E	L	I
U	T	E	R	I	N	G	S	U	R	T	M	N	W	L
S	A	R	T	S	N	O	P	Q	E	R	B	N	O	M
A	D	A	P	T	A	T	I	O	N	I	R	P	I	N
M	A	E	R	S	T	E	B	T	J	U	Y	W	T	A
V	G	H	T	E	R	A	I	N	E	T	O	E	Y	S
R	Y	T	O	P	M	K	O	I	L	M	R	W	O	T

Trees	_3_		1. Phototropism
Mitosis	___		2. Nucleus
Environment	___		3. Rings
Chloroplast	___		4. Protists
Virus	___		5. Cell division
Bacteria	___		6. Adaptation
Control center	___		7. Chlorophyll
Light response	___		8. Disease
Tissue	___		9. Muscle
Early organism	___		10. Embryo

130. Find the Endocrine System Pairs

★ The boxed words in the sentences below have pairs of letters missing. Read the sentence, then choose the correct missing pairs of letters from the Choice Box to complete the word. Sometimes only one letter is needed at the end of a word.

1. The endocrine system is called a | CO | | RO | | system.

2. The endocrine system regulates the | | TE | at which you grow.

3. The endocrine system consists of a series of | | AN | | .

4. The chemicals made in the endocrine glands are called | HO | | ON | | .

5. The | | TU | | AR | | gland produces several hormones, some of which control other glands.

6. The | TH | | OI | | gland in the neck controls the speed your body absorbs energy.

7. The four small glands that regulate the amount of calcium and other minerals in the blood are called the | | RA | | YR | | D | glands.

8. The | | NC | | AS | makes a hormone called insulin that helps the cells use sugar.

9. The adrenal glands produce a special emergency hormone called | AD | | NA | | N | .

10. The | | PR | | UC | | VE | glands are an important part of the endocrine system; they regulate sex-linked characteristics.

CHOICE BOX

PI	GL	PA	RE	Y	OD	TH	RM	ES	PA	RE	RA	NT	L	RE
				IT	YR	OI	D	DS	LI	TI				

131. Speedy Cell-Knowledge Puzzles

★ *Puzzle A:* Place a pair of letters into each set of empty spaces to complete the cell-related word or phrase.

1. __ __ cl __ __ s

2. ce __ __

3. __ __ ru __

4. __ __ ro __ __ so __ __

5. ge __ __

6. cy __ __ pl __ __ m

7. __ __ lo __ __ pl __ __ t

8. __ __ ll __ __ mb __ __ ne

★ *Puzzle B:* Each square contains an 8-letter cell-related word or phrase. Find the word by reading clockwise or counterclockwise. Each word or phrase starts at a different location. Spell it below.

C	E	L
L	■	L
L	A	W

M	B	R
E	■	A
M	E	N

U	C	A
O	■	V
L	E	S

M	O	R
S	■	G
I	N	A

_____   _____   _____   _____

★ *Puzzle C:* Unscramble the cell-related words and place them in the grid. A clue has been given at the end of each box.

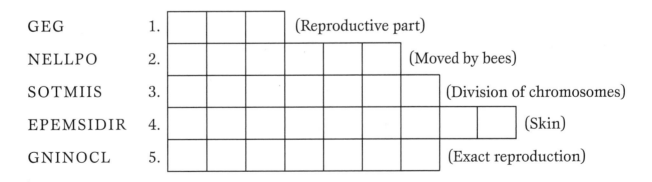

GEG   1. (Reproductive part)

NELLPO   2. (Moved by bees)

SOTMIIS   3. (Division of chromosomes)

EPEMSIDIR   4. (Skin)

GNINOCL   5. (Exact reproduction)

132. Life Science from Definitions and Context

★ **Choose a word from the definition set below that best describes what is occurring in each sentence.**

1. The plants in Akira's garden all pointed toward the sun. _____

2. When Akira cut down the apple tree, he could see the rings that indicated both poor and healthy growth. _____

3. The astronauts were happy to return to a place where they did not need their spacesuits. _____

4. Akira doesn't worry about bears in winter. _____

5. The ground is rich in the minerals plants need in order to grow.

   _____

6. Sonia and Akira lived on the prairies where they saw no trees.

   _____

7. Every year Sonia watched her pet geese fly south. _____

8. Sonia asked Akira if he knew of a butterfly that appeared similar to a Monarch.

   _____

DEFINITION SET

Dendrochronology: The science of studying the growth rings of trees.

Biosphere: The sphere or area of living things on Earth.

Fertile: Having the necessary elements for growth.

Grassland: A biome consisting mainly of grass vegetation.

Hibernation: A period of winter sleep for some animals.

Phototropism: The response of a plant to the position of the sun.

Instinct: Behavioral patterns that are not learned.

Mimicry: The ability of an organism to look like another.

133. Watch Out for Food Poisoning

★ One of the worst experiences you can go through in your life is to have food poisoning. The ill feelings, stomach cramps, and other problems are beyond belief and, therefore, to be avoided at all costs. Place the correct answer in the space provided that fits each description. A Choice Box has been given.

1. This type of poisoning is caused by improperly cooked food that has been canned, sealed, or preserved.

2. This type of poisoning is caused by eating food infected with the salmonella bacteria.

3. This type of poisoning is caused by people not washing hands before preparing food or from sneezing or coughing on food.

4. Another name for microorganism.

5. We need to wash our hands before eating or preparing food because many microorganisms live on this.

6. This is the general name for poisons produced by microorganisms in food.

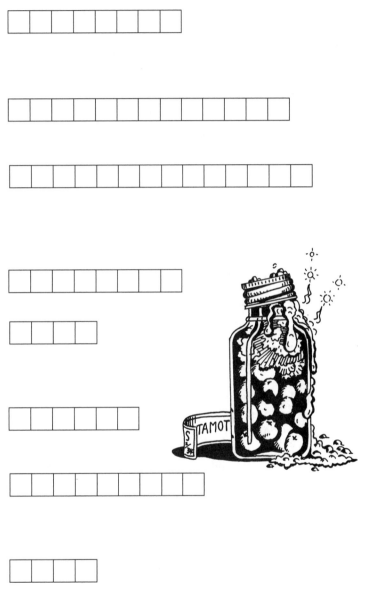

7. This is the name of the condition where food is trapped with no oxygen and harmful microorganisms are produced.

8. When foods like meat and poultry are left outside a fridge in this type of weather, food poisoning can occur.

CHOICE BOX

| staphylococcal | anaerobic | skin | warm |
| botulism | toxins | bacteria | salmonellosis |

134. Basic Plant Expressions from Clues and Scrambles

★ In Column 1 are clues to finding the plant word expressions you need for Column 3. Column 2 is the word you need for Column 3; however, it is scrambled. Place the unscrambled answer in Column 3.

Column 1—Clues	Column 2	Column 3
1. The science of studying tree rings.	LOORDNDECHRONOGY	_ _ _ _ _ _ _ _ _ _ _ _ _ _ _
2. A specialized reproductive cell that will create a new plant.	ROPSE	_ _ _ _ _
3. The male reproductive organ of a flower.	AMNSET	_ _ _ _ _ _
4. Part of the female reproductive organ of a flower.	ITSGAM	_ _ _ _ _ _
5. Fleshy underground stems that contain food for the plant.	EBUTRS	_ _ _ _ _ _
6. The process by which leaves give moisture to the atmosphere.	NSPIRNARTATIO	_ _ _ _ _ _ _ _ _ _ _ _ _
7. The process by which pollen is moved from the anther to stigma of a flower.	NOITLLOPINA	_ _ _ _ _ _ _ _ _ _ _
8. The process by which green plants build up carbohydrates by using water and carbon dioxide.	YSOTTNPHOHESIS	_ _ _ _ _ _ _ _ _ _ _ _ _
9. The process by which fluid travels through semipermeable membrane into solution of higher concentration.	OMSOSIS	_ _ _ _ _ _ _
10. An underground plant bud gorged with food.	ULBB	_ _ _ _
11. Plant growth as it responds to gravity.	OTRGEOPISM	_ _ _ _ _ _ _ _ _
12. Plant growth in response to the direction of the sun.	PRTOPHOTOISM	_ _ _ _ _ _ _ _ _ _ _

135. Microorganism Expressions from Clues and Scrambles

★ In Column 1 are the clues to finding the word you need for Column 3. Column 2 is the word you need for Column 3; however, it is scrambled. Write the circled letter in Column 4 to reveal the name of the fear some people have of microbes or bacteria.

Column 1	Column 2	Column 3	4
1. A microorganism scientist.	LOIBCGIORMOIST	_ _ _ _ _ O _ _ _ _ _ _ _ _	__
2. Whiplike structures with which some bacteria move.	LGAEFALL	_ _ O _ _ _ _ _	__
3. How bacteria grow on a solid surface.	OOYCLN	O _ _ _ _ _	__
4. These are smaller and simpler than bacteria.	SERSUVI	_ O _ _ _ _ _	__
5. Diatoms are the most common form of this.	GAALE	_ O _ _ _	__
6. All bacteria are __ or one celled.	LNSIGE	_ _ _ _ O _	__
7. Food poisoning caused by bacteria.	NALLELASMO	_ _ _ _ O _ _ _ _ _	__
8. This microbe causes malaria.	RTZOAOPO	O _ _ _ _ _ _ _	__
9. All organisms are in some way connected by the food __.	NIAHC	_ O _ _ _	__
10. A resting stage for bacteria.	EOSPR	_ _ O _ _	__
11. __ water kills bacteria.	GNIOBLI	O _ _ _ _ _ _	__
12. Free from microorganisms.	LRTSEIE	_ _ _ _ O _ _	__
13. Food must be prepared in these conditions.	LANCE	_ _ _ O _	__

The fear of microbes or bacteria is known as _____.

136. The Microorganism and Food Spiral

★ Place the answers to the microorganism and food questions into the spiral puzzle grid in their number order. Be careful! Some answers may overlap. A Choice Box has been provided.

Food that has been invaded by micro-organisms may be (1) _____.

(2) _____ is caused by bacteria found in soil.

The (3) _____ bacteria causes salmonellosis.

Microscopic yeast cells cause (4) _____, which could result in wine. Microorganisms need to be deprived of (5) _____ or (6) _____ or (7) _____ to prevent growth of harmful bacteria.

The modern food industry relies on chemical (8) _____ to control bacteria growth.

(9) _____ is a cold way to preserve food.

(10) _____ foods were used by the Emperor Napoleon of France to preserve food for his soldiers.

The bacteria-killing process of (11) _____ is named after Louis Pasteur.

Food must be kept clean to avoid all kinds of (12) _____, as well as bacteria.

CHOICE BOX

oxygen	pasteurization	salmonella	fermentation	canned	freezing
botulism	additives	moisture	contaminants	poisonous	heat

137. Life Science Controversies: Part One

★ Read each statement. Circle "Yes" if you agree with, or support, the statement. Circle "No" if you disagree with, or do not support, the statement. Then write why you agree or disagree with each statement. (These may be used for class discussions.)

1. There should be a ban on cloning of humans.   YES   NO

_____

_____

_____

2. Who cares about global warming? It's better to be warm than to freeze.   YES   NO

_____

_____

_____

3. There is no need to recycle paper. There are plenty of trees around—just look at our forests.   YES   NO

_____

_____

_____

4. There is no harm in people hunting wild animals because animals hunt and kill each other all the time.   YES   NO

_____

_____

_____

5. Evolution doesn't appear to be logical. How could something evolve from nothing in the first place?   YES   NO

_____

_____

_____

138. Life Science Controversies: Part Two

★ Read each statement. Circle "Yes" if you agree with, or support, the statement. Circle "No" if you disagree with, or do not support, the statement. Then write why you agree or disagree with each statement. (These may be used for class discussions.)

1. People should not cut trees, especially with an axe, because trees have feelings.   YES   NO

   _____

   _____

   _____

2. Drilling for oil on the ocean floor has no harmful effect on the environment.   YES   NO

   _____

   _____

   _____

3. Junk food should be banned from school cafeterias and vending machines.   YES   NO

   _____

   _____

   _____

4. Farm animals should be allowed to roam free in pastures instead of being penned in feedlots and coops.   YES   NO

   _____

   _____

   _____

5. All travelers returning from foreign countries should be made to sterilize their footwear to prevent the spread of harmful bacteria.   YES   NO

   _____

   _____

   _____

139. Nervous System and Endocrine "Not the Same As" Vocabulary

★ Read each sentence starter below. Each one states that one nervous system and endocrine-related thing is not the same as another. Your task is to explain how they are different.

1. Central nervous system is not the same as peripheral nervous system because

_____

2. Voluntary responses are not the same as involuntary responses because _____

_____

3. Sensory nerve cells are not the same as motor nerve cells because _____

_____

4. Reflex is not the same as learned response because _____

_____

5. Brain is not the same as spinal cord because _____

_____

6. Cerebellum is not the same as cerebrum because _____

_____

7. Paralysis is not the same as movement because _____

_____

8. Pancreas is not the same as hormones because _____

_____

9. Dwarfism is not the same as giantism because _____

_____

10. Adrenal glands are not the same as thyroid glands because _____

_____

140. Life Organisms: Eliminating the Negative and Explaining "Why"

★ This assignment is unusual because you are *not* to choose the correct answer to fit into the space in each sentence. Instead, *you must choose (circle) the least correct answer*. There are three possible answers at the end of each sentence. One is absolutely correct or true, one could be true, and one is false or incorrect. You must explain *why* the answer you circled is completely wrong or incorrect, or how it does not fit the context of the sentence.

1. ____ are made up of material developed into living systems.
   (Organisms, Amoeba, Microscope)

   _____

   _____

2. ____ are the fundamental basic units of life. **(Protoplasm, Cells, Antibodies)**

   _____

   _____

3. Cells are generated only by ____ organisms. **(genetic, living, environmental)**

   _____

   _____

4. As long as ____ is present, life will continue in an organism.
   (vitality, mitosis, energy)

   _____

   _____

5. Most organisms possess a distinct ____ that is common to its species.
   (life span, growth rate, marketing process)

   _____

   _____

6. Growth is a function of a set of ____ processes.
   (chemical, biological, polluted)

   _____

   _____

7. Organisms must ____ if life is to continue. **(breathe, reproduce, run)**

   _____

   _____

8. All organisms act, react, and are governed by their ____.
   (phototropism, environment, organ systems)

   _____

   _____

141. Life Sciences Speculation and Information: Part One

★ On line A, describe what you think the word or expression means.

★ On line B, give the dictionary or glossary definition of the word or expression.

1. Migration   (A) _____

                (B) _____

2. Mimicry   (A) _____

                (B) _____

3. Phototropism   (A) _____

                (B) _____

4. Protective coloration   (A) _____

                (B) _____

5. Environment   (A) _____

                (B) _____

6. Adaptation   (A) _____

                (B) _____

7. Biological clock   (A) _____

                (B) _____

8. Instinct   (A) _____

                (B) _____

142. Life Sciences Speculation and Information: Part Two

★   On line A, describe what you think the word or expression means.

★   On line B, give the dictionary or glossary definition of the word or expression.

1. Cold-blooded
(A) _____
(B) _____

2. Imprinting
(A) _____
(B) _____

3. Genetically modified organism
(A) _____
(B) _____

4. Climate
(A) _____
(B) _____

5. Hibernation
(A) _____
(B) _____

6. Breeding grounds
(A) _____
(B) _____

7. Life cycle
(A) _____
(B) _____

8. Food chain
(A) _____
(B) _____

143. All About the Biosphere/Biome

★ Look at the Choice Box. Find the word that should appear in each numbered blank space in the paragraphs. Write that word on the numbered line at the left. No word may be used more than once.

1. _____
2. _____
3. _____
4. _____
5. _____
6. _____
7. _____
8. _____
9. _____
10. _____
11. _____
12. _____
13. _____
14. _____
15. _____
16. _____
17. _____
18. _____
19. _____
20. _____

All living __1__ need a safe __2__ in which to survive and __3__. Different __4__ of plants and animals exist in different places by __5__ to their __6__. The basic __7__ or conditions for life for any organism in any environment are __8__, water, __9__, room to live, and a proper __10__. These elements or __11__, for the most part, exist in a small area just below the planet's surface, at the __12__, and in the air above the surface. This living __13__ is called the __14__.

The amount of basic elements or conditions for __15__ are not evenly __16__ on the Earth. Therefore, different types of __17__ and animals must adapt to conditions as they are in different places. The different places with differing conditions are known as life zones or __18__. It can be said that a biome is a __19__ environment where animals and plants with similar __20__ can exist together and multiply.

CHOICE BOX

distributed	region	biomes	surface	plants
food	climate	elements	air	biosphere
multiply	types	conditions	adapting	survival
environment	safe	organisms	surroundings	needs

144. The Biome, or Life Zone: Part One

★ A biome, or life zone, is an environment on Earth where the same kinds of organisms can survive. On the left are the names of three biomes. Your task is to choose six appropriate elements, situations, or living organisms from the Choice Box to suit each one. Some items in the Choice Box may be appropriate for each biome.

Tundra _____   _____

_____   _____

_____   _____

The Taiga (Swamp Forest) _____   _____

_____   _____

_____   _____

The Deciduous Forest _____   _____

_____   _____

_____   _____

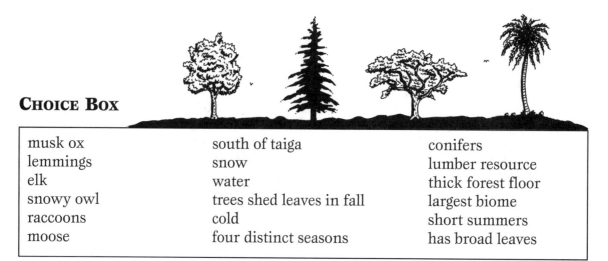

CHOICE BOX

musk ox	south of taiga	conifers
lemmings	snow	lumber resource
elk	water	thick forest floor
snowy owl	trees shed leaves in fall	largest biome
raccoons	cold	short summers
moose	four distinct seasons	has broad leaves

145. The Biome, or Life Zone: Part Two

★ A biome, or life zone, is an environment on Earth where the same kind of organisms can survive. On the left are the names of three biomes. Your task is to choose six appropriate elements, situations, or living organisms from the Choice Box to suit each one. Some items in the Choice Box may be appropriate for each biome.

The Desert _____ _____

_____ _____

_____ _____

The Grassland _____ _____

_____ _____

_____ _____

The Tropical Forest _____ _____

_____ _____

_____ _____

CHOICE BOX

water	summers hot, winters cold	dry	sagebrush
lizards	swimming snakes and lizards	alligators	called prairie
snakes	deep dark fertile soil	undiscovered plants	largest is Sahara
cactus	hot by day, cold at night	cattle and sheep graze	cereal crops grown
orchids	green foliage all year	tall grasses	quick evaporation
	richest in plants and animals		

146. Life Science Vocabulary Vowelless Puzzle

★ Listed in the Choice Box are some of the most important words associated with Life Science. Your task is to find the correct Life Science words in the puzzle. All the vowels (A, E, I, O, U, Y) have been removed. You will need to write the vowels in place as you find the words.

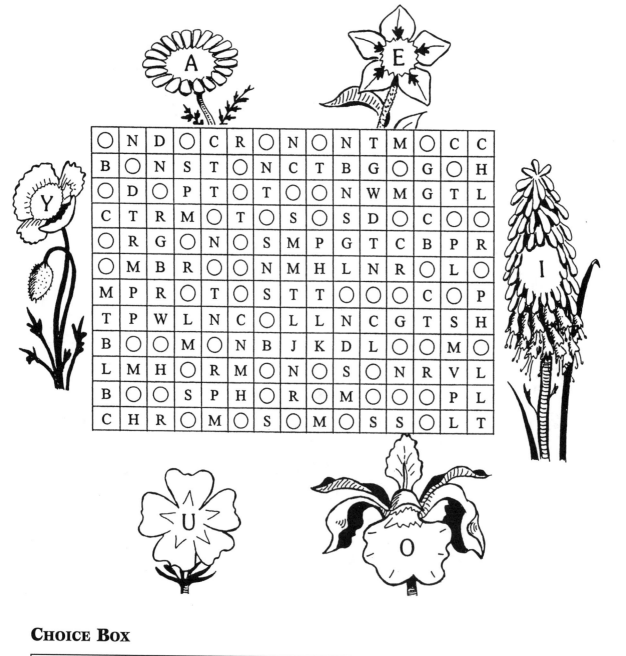

CHOICE BOX

GENES	BIOSPHERE	EGG	NUCLEUS	PROTIST
ADAPTATION	CELL	EMBRYO	ENDOCRINE	BIOME
MITOSIS	CHLOROPHYLL	HORMONES	INSTINCT	GLAND
BACTERIA	CHROMOSOMES	MIMICRY	ORGANISM	CYTOPLASM

147. Life Science's Odd One Out

★ Find the word in each Life Science group that does not belong. Write that word in the space provided. Be careful! Words become more difficult as you near the bottom of the page.

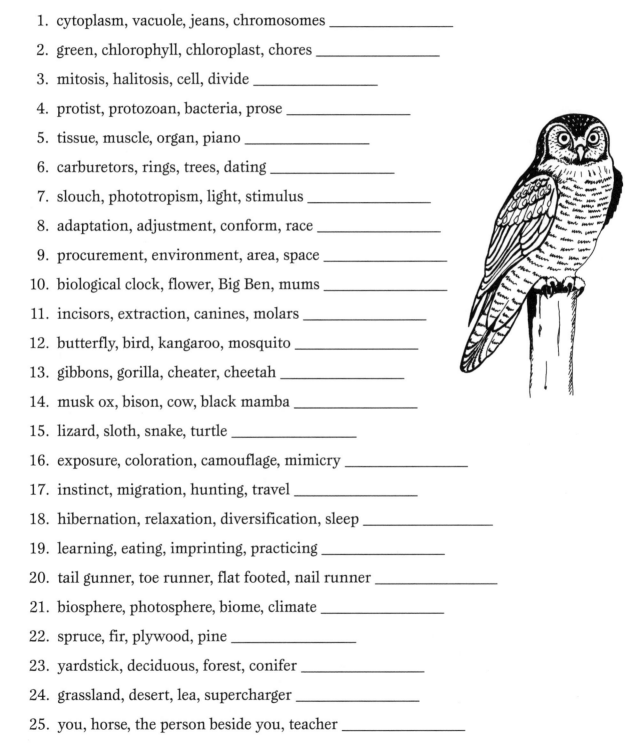

1. cytoplasm, vacuole, jeans, chromosomes _____

2. green, chlorophyll, chloroplast, chores _____

3. mitosis, halitosis, cell, divide _____

4. protist, protozoan, bacteria, prose _____

5. tissue, muscle, organ, piano _____

6. carburetors, rings, trees, dating _____

7. slouch, phototropism, light, stimulus _____

8. adaptation, adjustment, conform, race _____

9. procurement, environment, area, space _____

10. biological clock, flower, Big Ben, mums _____

11. incisors, extraction, canines, molars _____

12. butterfly, bird, kangaroo, mosquito _____

13. gibbons, gorilla, cheater, cheetah _____

14. musk ox, bison, cow, black mamba _____

15. lizard, sloth, snake, turtle _____

16. exposure, coloration, camouflage, mimicry _____

17. instinct, migration, hunting, travel _____

18. hibernation, relaxation, diversification, sleep _____

19. learning, eating, imprinting, practicing _____

20. tail gunner, toe runner, flat footed, nail runner _____

21. biosphere, photosphere, biome, climate _____

22. spruce, fir, plywood, pine _____

23. yardstick, deciduous, forest, conifer _____

24. grassland, desert, lea, supercharger _____

25. you, horse, the person beside you, teacher _____

148. Plant World Tripod Connections

★   Listed below are 14 sets of three words that all have something in common
    in the plant world. Identify what they have in common and write your
    answer in the space provided. A dictionary or glossary will help.

1.   seed   stamen   spore   _____

2.   annual   perennial   cycle   _____

3.   chlorophyll   green plants   magnesium   _____

4.   ring   year   bark   _____

5.   flower   bee   pollen   _____

6.   deciduous   branches   limb   _____

7.   corn   peas   carrots   _____

8.   bulb   seed   spore   _____

9.   sugar   cellulose   starch   _____

10. leaves   flowers   bark   _____

11. phototropism   hydrotropism   geotropism   _____

12. peas   beans   lupines   _____

13. light   water   nutrients   _____

14. water   membrane   permeable   _____

Copyright © 2003 by John Wiley & Sons, Inc.

149. Adaptation of Colorization and Shape

★ Find the word that should appear in each numbered blank space in the paragraphs. Write that word on the numbered line at the left. A Choice Box has been provided.

QUICK ACCESS
information

1. _____

2. _____

3. _____

4. _____

5. _____

6. _____

7. _____

8. _____

9. _____

10. _____

11. _____

12. _____

13. _____

14. _____

15. _____

16. _____

17. _____

18. _____

19. _____

20. _____

Many animals have a _1_ way of _2_ themselves or _3_ themselves for hunting. They change their _4_ to blend into their background or _5_ . This makes it _6_ to see them. The chameleon lizard is the most famous example of this. The chameleon will turn _7_ when on a black branch, or green when on a green leaf. The polar bear _8_ change its coloration like the chameleon. The polar bear has _9_ fur _10_ year long. This is said to be a _11_ camouflage. It prevents the polar bear from being _12_ noticed against the _13_ of its environment.

Some animals' bodies are _14_ to look _15_ to their surroundings. The _16_ of some butterflies are shaped like the leaves they rest or feed on. This is called protective _17_ .

Other animals use _18_ to look like _19_ or dangerous animals. The viceroy butterfly looks like a monarch butterfly that is poisonous to birds. When birds see the viceroy, they think it is a _20_ and will not eat it.

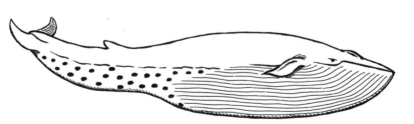

CHOICE BOX

environment	similar	unique	shaped	easily
wings	mimicry	black	coloration	protecting
doesn't	monarch	disguising	resemblance	snow
white	natural	poisonous	difficult	all

150. Life Science Search from Clues

★ The partially spelled Life Science words, phrases, and terms below are related to or defined by the information or clue under each one. Your task is to complete the word, phrase, or term using the data or clues. A Choice Box has been provided.

1. _ _ _ _ M _ S _ _ E _
   (*blueprints of the cell*)

2. C_ _ _   D_ _ _ _ _ _ _ _
   (*how some organisms grow larger*)

3. A_ _ _ I _ _ _ _ _ _
   (*dependence on a drug*)

4. H _ _ M _ _ _ _
   (*these regulate many body activities*)

5. _ _ R _ _ _ _
   (*soft-cavity center of bones*)

6. _ RO _ _ _ _ _ _ _ _ _
   (*growing new plants from plant parts*)

7. _ _ _ R_ _   _ _ RM_ _ _ _ _
   (*how yeast reproduces*)

8. A_ _ _ _ _ _ _
   _ EP_ _ _ _ _ _ _ _ _ _
   (*nonsexual reproduction*)

9. _ _ _ E _
   (*the formations on chromosomes that determine heredity traits*)

10. C_ _ R _ _ _ _
    (*a person who has a gene for a trait but does not show it*)

11. _ _ _ _RAL   _ _ _ECTIO_
    (*nature's heredity selection process*)

12. _ _ N _ _ _ _ _
    (*the study of the processes of heredity*)

13. _ _ _ _ _ _L
    (*evidence of an organism that once lived*)

14. A _ _ _ _ _ _ T _ _ _ _
    (*the ability to survive in an environment*)

15. E_ _ SY _ _ _ _ _
    (*a set of organisms in their environment*)

16. F_ _ _   C_ _ _ _ _
    (*the passing of energy in the form of food*)

17. _ _ _ RY _
    (*a divided fertilized egg*)

18. _ _ LL _ _ _ _ _ _ _ _
    (*the transfer of pollen from anther to stigma*)

19. _ _ _O_ _I _ _   G_ _ _DS
    (*where hormones are made*)

20. C _ REB_ _ _ _
    (*the largest area of the brain*)

21. _N_ _ _ _ _ _ _ _R_
    M _ _ _ _ _ _ _
    (*muscles you do not control*)

22. V _ _ _ _ _ TAR_
    M _ _ _ _ _ _ _
    (*muscles you do control*)

23. _ IG _ _ _ _ _ S
    (*connecting tissue in the body*)

24. _ AR _ _ _ O _ _
    (*an organism that eats only animal tissue*)

25. H _ _ ED _ _ _ _
    (*the passing of traits from parent to offspring*)

CHOICE BOX

ENDOCRINE GLANDS	CELL DIVISION	CEREBRUM	ADDICTION	SPORE FORMATION
PROPAGATION	HORMONES	MARROW	LIGAMENTS	CHROMOSOMES
ASEXUAL REPRODUCTION	POLLINATION	EMBRYO	GENES	VOLUNTARY MUSCLES
INVOLUNTARY MUSCLES	HEREDITY	FOOD CHAIN	ECOSYSTEM	ADAPTATION
NATURAL SELECTION	CARNIVORE	FOSSIL	CARRIER	GENETICS

NAME _____   DATE _____

151. How One Life Form Is Like Another: Part One

★   Many life forms have similarities, even though at first they may appear to be very different. Your task is to describe how the first item (A) is somehow like the second item (B). Be sure to use complete, proper sentences for your answers.

1. (A)   Shark   (B)   Whale

_____

_____

2. (A)   Panda Bear   (B)   Grizzly Bear

_____

_____

3. (A)   Tiger   (B)   House cat

_____

_____

4. (A)   Flamingo   (B)   Sparrow

_____

_____

5. (A)   Rattlesnake   (B)   Worm

_____

_____

6. (A)   Tarantula   (B)   Scorpion

_____

_____

7. (A)   Housefly   (B)   Dragonfly

_____

_____

8. (A)   Frog   (B)   Toad

_____

_____

152. How One Life Form Is Like Another: Part Two

★ Many life forms have similarities, even though at first they may appear to be very different. Your task is to describe how the first item (A) is somehow like the second item (B). Be sure to use complete, proper sentences for your answers.

1. (A)   Ancient Dinosaurs   (B)   American Alligator of today

_____

_____

2. (A)   Chicken   (B)   Turkey

_____

_____

3. (A)   Elk   (B)   Deer

_____

_____

4. (A)   Horse   (B)   Donkey

_____

_____

5. (A)   Bat   (B)   Bird

_____

_____

6. (A)   Chimpanzee   (B)   Gorilla

_____

_____

7. (A)   Rat   (B)   Squirrel

_____

_____

8. (A)   Hare   (B)   Kangaroo

_____

_____

NAME _____   DATE _____

153. How One Life Form Is <u>Not</u> Like Another: Part One

★ Many life forms have differences, even though they may be connected in some way. Your task is to describe how the two items in each line differ. Resource materials (encyclopedia) may be required. Be sure to use complete, proper sentences for your answers.

1. Rabbit, Hare _____
_____

2. Porcupine, Skunk _____
_____

3. Dog, Wolf _____
_____

4. Dolphin, Whale _____
_____

5. Alligator, Crocodile _____
_____

6. Kangaroo, Wallaby _____
_____

7. Leopard, Cheetah _____
_____

8. Lion, Tiger _____
_____

9. Walrus, Seal _____
_____

10. Rhinoceros, Hippopotamus _____
_____

154. How One Life Form Is <u>Not</u> Like Another: Part Two

★ Many life forms have differences, even though they may be connected in some way. Your task is to describe how the two items in each line differ. Resource materials (encyclopedia) may be required. Be sure to use complete, proper sentences for your answers.

1. Horse, Zebra _____

_____

2. Cow, Elephant _____

_____

3. Bactrian Camel, Dromedary _____

_____

4. Buffalo, Deer _____

_____

5. Butterfly, Moth _____

_____

6. Turtle, Tortoise _____

_____

7. Dodo bird, Eagle _____

_____

8. Lobster, Crab _____

_____

9. Flea, Tick _____

_____

10. Ostrich, Emu _____

_____

155. A Resources Puzzle

★   Read the clues to the resources puzzle and place the answers in their correct
    locations on the puzzle.

1. Materials that we use from
   the earth are called natural
   ____.

2. When a resource can be
   replaced naturally, it is said
   to be a ____ resource.

3. A forest resource.

4. Today, many trees are grown
   on tree ____.

5. The name of a living and
   moving organism that is not a
   plant or bacteria.

6. Because of over-hunting,
   some animals no longer ____.

7. As the Earth's population
   ____, natural resources are
   used faster.

8. Our greatest liquid resource.

9. The resource we breathe.

10. The amount of water we
    have is renewed in a water
    ____.

11. When soil is rich in minerals
    and food ingredients, it is
    said to be ____.

12. These resources cannot be
    made new or replaced.

SECTION 8

WATER AND EROSION FACTS AND INSIGHTS

156. How to Find Gold and Become Rich

★ Find the word that should appear in each numbered blank in the paragraph. Write the words on the numbered blanks on the left. A Choice Box has been provided.

1. _____

2. _____

3. _____

4. _____

5. _____

6. _____

7. _____

8. _____

9. _____

10. _____

11. _____

12. _____

13. _____

14. _____

15. _____

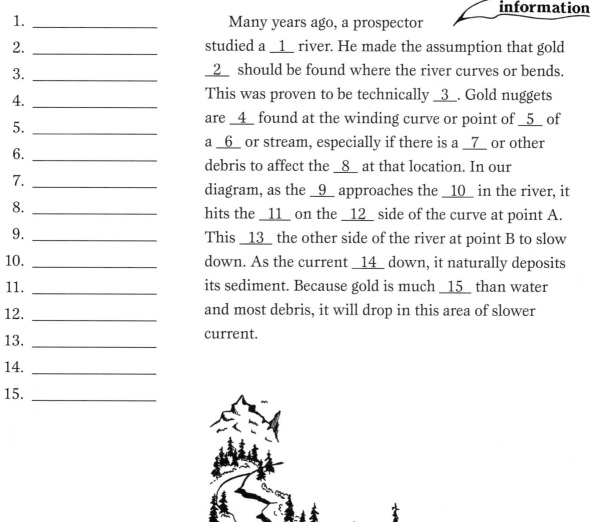

QUICK ACCESS information

Many years ago, a prospector studied a __1__ river. He made the assumption that gold __2__ should be found where the river curves or bends. This was proven to be technically __3__. Gold nuggets are __4__ found at the winding curve or point of __5__ of a __6__ or stream, especially if there is a __7__ or other debris to affect the __8__ at that location. In our diagram, as the __9__ approaches the __10__ in the river, it hits the __11__ on the __12__ side of the curve at point A. This __13__ the other side of the river at point B to slow down. As the current __14__ down, it naturally deposits its sediment. Because gold is much __15__ than water and most debris, it will drop in this area of slower current.

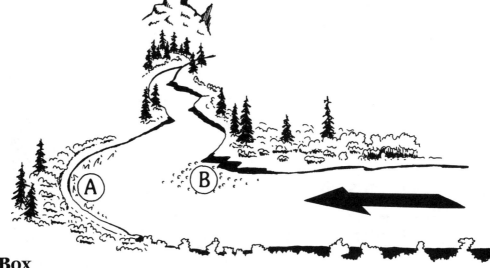

CHOICE BOX

nuggets	bend	far	meander	often
tree	denser	river	bank	correct
water	causes	slows	winding	current

157. A Hydrosphere Puzzle

★ Use the clues from the sentences to fill in the missing letters in the puzzle grid. The word you need is scrambled after each sentence.

1. The ____ consists of all types of water formation on Earth.
   RYOPEHSDHRE

2. A ____ is a massive frozen ice block that once moved on the Earth in the Ice Age. **LCIEAGR**

3. ____ ____ is a gaseous form of water. **AEVAPWTROR**

4. ____ is liquid condensation on grass on a summer morning. **WED**

5. The term ____ refers to all swimming life forms. **ETNOKN**

6. ____ are free-floating tiny organisms that drift with the ocean current.
   NOTKNALP

7. ____ are a type of algae and make up the main food source for some animals.
   ATOMSID

8. ____ are bottom-dwelling sea creatures. **ENOSBTH**

9. ____ is where the land and sea meet. **LINEROSHE**

10. Sea water has a large amount of ____. **ASLT**

1.	H		D		O		P				E
2.		L		I		R	
3.		A		E	R			P	O	
4.	D	
5.		E		T		
6.	P		A		K			N
7.			A		O		S	
8.		E			H	O	
9.		H			E		I		E
10.			L		

158. All About Erosion

★ Use only the letters in the box to find the words needed to fill in the blanks. Some letters are used more than once.

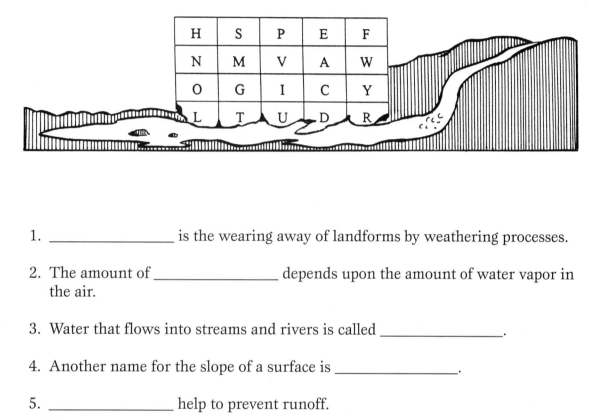

H	S	P	E	F
N	M	V	A	W
O	G	I	C	Y
L	T	U	D	R

1. _____ is the wearing away of landforms by weathering processes.

2. The amount of _____ depends upon the amount of water vapor in the air.

3. Water that flows into streams and rivers is called _____.

4. Another name for the slope of a surface is _____.

5. _____ help to prevent runoff.

6. _____ rocks allow water to enter the ground.

7. _____ are a large violent form of erosion.

8. _____ is a slow erosion on a hillside in a humid climate.

9. Freezing and _____ create loose rock areas that fall away.

10. When a river develops curves, it is said to be _____.

159. Double-Sided Erosion Synonyms

★ Listed below are 17 words related to erosion. You are to find their synonyms (words that mean the same or nearly the same). The words to be found in Puzzle A have synonyms in Puzzle B. The words and their synonyms begin at the same place in each puzzle, but some words have longer or shorter synonyms.

★ Circle the word in either Puzzle A or B and then circle its synonym in the other puzzle.

★ Write the correct synonyms next to the words listed below. Some are found in Puzzle A and some are found in Puzzle B. One is done for you to help you get started.

Puzzle A

D	R	Y	E	B	T	Y	S	T	R	E	A	M
S	U	S	L	O	P	E	N	M	K	D	F	P
H	W	I	N	D	E	R	W	D	I	R	L	E
O	A	S	E	T	D	F	E	G	N	I	O	B
R	M	E	A	N	D	E	R	A	E	P	W	B
E	A	S	E	T	Y	J	L	K	W	A	E	L
L	W	S	I	L	T	D	E	F	T	B	L	E
I	F	L	O	O	D	E	L	D	K	P	W	O
N	T	U	R	B	U	L	E	N	C	E	O	L
E	D	G	V	A	S	P	E	M	U	R	K	Y
M	I	W	R	E	T	X	C	E	R	O	D	E
M	E	L	T	C	A	N	D	Y	O	V	E	L
C	A	N	Y	O	N	L	E	T	D	I	R	T

Puzzle B

A	R	I	D	L	O	P	C	R	E	E	K	O
B	C	I	N	C	L	I	N	E	A	T	R	S
E	B	R	E	E	Z	E	Y	T	R	R	U	T
A	F	R	D	S	A	E	B	T	A	I	N	O
C	C	U	R	V	E	A	S	E	R	C	O	N
H	F	H	I	L	P	O	M	V	E	K	F	E
L	O	S	E	D	I	M	E	N	T	L	F	T
E	O	V	E	R	F	L	O	W	C	E	B	E
V	S	T	O	R	M	C	E	T	L	O	P	G
C	Y	S	T	R	O	V	B	M	U	D	D	Y
E	D	I	P	L	W	E	S	D	E	C	A	Y
D	E	F	R	O	S	T	T	Y	O	P	E	R
G	O	R	G	E	R	E	W	A	S	O	I	L

1. slope _____

2. stream _____

3. pebble _____

4. dry _____arid_____

5. canyon _____

6. shoreline _____

7. wind _____

8. soil _____

9. sediment _____

10. defrost _____

11. storm _____

12. flood _____

13. runoff _____

14. trickle _____

15. erode _____

16. muddy _____

17. meander _____

NAME _____ DATE _____

160. A Two-Space Water Puzzle

★ Water is so common that all of us take it for granted. It is necessary to study water because of its importance to all life forms and its strange properties. Fill in the two blanks in each sentence using words from the Choice Box.

1. Pure water is _____, odorless, and _____.

2. Pure water consists of the elements _____ and _____.

3. The process of decomposing water by passing an _____ current through it is called _____.

4. Water exists in nature in three states: _____, liquid, and _____.

5. Of the 70% of the Earth's surface covered by water, 97% is _____ water which is mainly in the _____.

6. One very strange property of water is its ability to _____ or become less _____ in a solid state than in a liquid state.

7. 98% of _____ water on Earth is locked in the _____ ice caps.

8. Many _____ like lettuce, tomatoes, and spinach are over _____ water.

9. The average human requires about _____ liters of water per _____ if all forms are considered.

10. More fresh water is being _____ from its sources than is being _____ through the water cycle.

CHOICE BOX

oceans	gas	colorless	fresh	replenished
expand	polar	removed	90%	solid
hydrogen	tasteless	oxygen	8,500	salt
electrolysis	vegetables	electric	day	dense

161. Liquid "Not the Same As" Vocabulary

★ Read each sentence starter below. Each one states that one liquid-related thing is not the same as another. Your task is to explain how they are different.

1. A <u>solution</u> is not the same as a <u>mixture</u> because _____
_____

2. <u>Water</u> is not the same as <u>ice</u> because _____
_____

3. <u>Solute</u> is not the same as <u>solvent</u> because _____
_____

4. <u>Homogenous</u> is not the same as <u>heterogenous</u> because _____
_____

5. <u>Water vapor</u> is not the same as <u>oxygen</u> because _____
_____

6. An <u>aquifer</u> is not the same as a <u>reservoir</u> because _____
_____

7. <u>Ocean water</u> is not the same as <u>Great Lakes water</u> because _____
_____

8. <u>Diluted</u> is not the same as <u>concentrated</u> because _____
_____

9. <u>Saturated</u> is not the same as <u>unsaturated</u> because _____
_____

10. <u>Solubility</u> is not the same as <u>permeability</u> because _____
_____

162. Hydrology Vocabulary

★ **At the end of each sentence, write a word or phrase from the Choice Box that is described by the underlined words.**

1. Tours are made by huge four-wheel-drive vehicles onto <u>large blocks or slabs of ice hundreds of feet thick</u> that once moved inch by inch across the land. _____

2. Below the ground is <u>a large amount of moisture just below the surface that varies in content with a wet or dry climate.</u> _____

3. <u>This is a large amount of liquid H_2O concentrated at the uppermost area of the topography.</u> _____

4. This is the name of a <u>small depression in the landscape containing a non-mobile hydrological substance.</u> _____

5. This is the name given to <u>a metamorphic, igneous, or sedimentary formation that possesses water.</u> _____

6. This is the name of <u>a wide tidal-influenced river mouth that can contain both fresh and salt water.</u> _____

7. This is the name of a <u>huge block of floating ice that sank the unsinkable ship.</u> _____

8. This is the name of the <u>hydrological entity that regularly emits a vapor and liquid form of H_2O</u> in Yellowstone National Park. _____

CHOICE BOX

surface water	ground water	iceberg	Old Faithful geyser
aquifer	estuary	slough	glaciers

163. Erosion: Eliminating the Negative and Explaining "Why"

★ This assignment is unusual because you are *not* to choose the correct answer to fit into the space in each sentence. Instead, *you must choose (circle) the least correct answer*. There are three possible answers at the end of each sentence. One is absolutely correct or true, one could be true, and one is false or incorrect. You must explain *why* the answer you circled is completely wrong or incorrect, or how it does not fit the context of the sentence.

1. In ____ regions, runoff from torrential rainfalls is normally fast.
   (tropical, dry, arid)

   _____

   _____

2. Sand ____ are created by continually blowing sand. **(oasis, dunes, drifts)**

   _____

   _____

3. The name for the erosion deposits seen at the foot of slopes is ____.
   (talus, till, talcum)

   _____

   _____

4. The name of the water in the water table is ____.
   (ground water, subterranean hydrology, capillaries)

   _____

   _____

5. Porous rocks are ____. **(permanent, penetrable, permeable)**

   _____

   _____

6. ____ are rocks that allow free movement of underground water.
   (Artesian areas, Aquifers, Aqueducts)

   _____

   _____

7. A flat-topped hill called a(n) ____ is very common in the arid and semi-arid regions of the U.S. **(mesa, butte, estuary)**

   _____

   _____

164. Let's Tackle the Hydrosphere

★   Run left to right on this football field by unscrambling the hydrosphere-
related words. Score 7 points every time you reach the touchdown end zone.

**7-Point
Touchdown
End Zone**

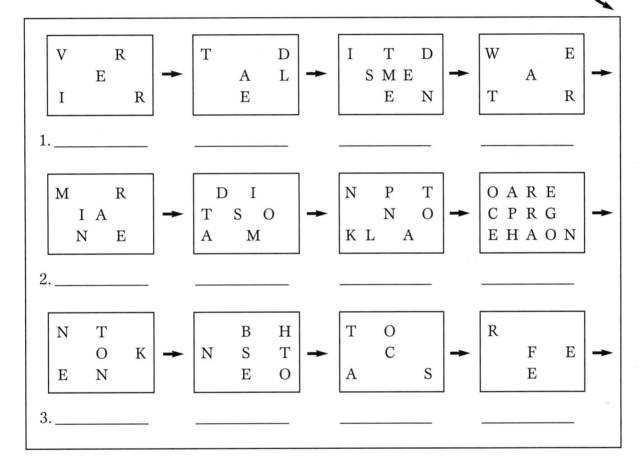

1. _____   _____   _____   _____

2. _____   _____   _____   _____

3. _____   _____   _____   _____

Field Goal: The name given to the deepest part of the ocean is the _____.
(This field goal is worth 3 points if you get it correct!)

_____
Total Points

165. A Water-Properties Spiral

★ On the left are 12 important properties of water. Think of the word that will complete each sentence and write that word in its correct number location in the puzzle.

1. Water _____ at 0° C.

2. Water has a high surface _____.

3. Water _____ during freezing.

4. Pure water is _____.

5. Water is a poor wetting agent. It does not _____ to solids well.

6. Water has a high _____ capacity.

7. Water _____ heat quickly from objects immersed in it.

8. Large amounts of water affect the _____ temperature around it.

9. Water can _____ as a gas, liquid, or solid.

10. Ice has a relatively high _____ point.

11. Water has a relatively _____ boiling point.

12. Much of the water on Earth is in a state of _____ change.

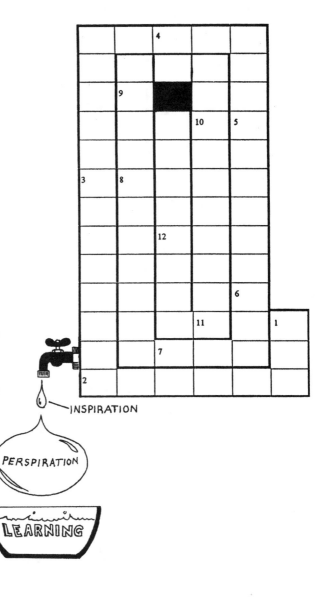

INSPIRATION

PERSPIRATION

LEARNING

NAME _____   DATE _____

166. "Sea" the Ocean

★   Use the clues to fill in the missing letters on the grid. The word you need is
scrambled after each sentence.

1. The process of following a path or course on the open sea.
   OIGIVNAATN

2. The name for the worldwide change in sea level.   **ASUETSY**

3. The name for the flowing motion of the sea.   **TURNRCES**

4. The amount of salt in the oceans is its degree of this.   **NIITASLY**

5. An ocean volcano with a flat top below the ocean's surface.   **TYGUO**

6. A valley on the ocean floor.   **RNHCTE**

7. This occurs when water rises to the surface from the sea floor.
   WLLNIUPEG

8. The rise and fall of the world's water level due to lunar forces.   **EDTI**

9. Even waves that move across the ocean.   **LESWL**

10. A favorite of surfers, its wave top curves and crashes toward shore.
    RKEBRAE

1.	N			I							
2.		U		A							
3.			R	R							
4.			L								
5.				T							
6.	T			H							
7.		P				G					
8.		D									
9.		E									
10.		R									

167. Erosion Adjectives

In our study of erosion, we look at many things, processes, and systems that can be better understood if we can describe aspects of each one.

★   Use <u>adjectives</u> to describe the following <u>things</u> associated with erosion.

(1) Flood Plain	(2) Aquifer	(3) Avalanche
(4) Water Table	(5) Delta	(6) Geyser

★   Use <u>adjectives</u> to describe the following <u>processes</u> and <u>systems</u> associated with erosion.

(1) Meander	(2) Runoff	(3) Landslide
(4) Creep	(5) Capillary Action	(6) Saturation

168. The Erosion Wordsearch

★ Locate and circle the answers to the erosion clues in the grid. The answers have been provided after the clues; however, they are scrambled. Study the clue, then decipher the word.

G	S	L	A	N	D	S	L	I	D	E	K	R	C	F	R	S	A	T	T
R	T	A	T	H	W	Y	S	T	H	A	T	S	E	L	H	P	V	R	R
A	U	X	S	D	E	G	Y	S	E	T	Y	W	S	O	U	R	O	E	I
D	F	T	U	P	W	I	G	K	L	E	C	A	H	O	P	I	R	K	B
I	J	W	R	E	D	E	R	U	N	O	F	F	R	D	O	N	S	T	U
E	O	D	G	H	R	Y	P	O	L	K	E	R	E	P	L	G	E	R	T
N	S	O	M	E	A	N	D	E	R	E	R	I	L	L	K	S	H	J	A
T	T	V	O	L	I	G	J	L	E	R	I	L	J	A	O	B	E	R	R
N	O	R	U	M	N	L	G	E	Y	S	E	R	H	I	M	D	T	H	I
X	E	I	E	S	A	W	R	E	B	W	O	R	O	N	O	E	A	E	E
T	H	V	R	S	G	T	T	R	E	A	W	S	N	R	P	L	R	T	S
R	L	E	V	E	E	W	A	Q	U	I	F	E	R	S	E	T	X	A	S
S	C	R	R	I	C	T	H	E	J	X	O	T	S	I	T	A	E	T	H

ACROSS

1. Water that flows on or near the surface in rivers, streams, and brooks. **(NOFRUF)**
2. A rapid movement of rock down a mountainside. **(DDNLASLIE)**
3. An S-shaped curve in a river. **(NDAMEER)**
4. A natural or hand-built mound that contains a river or stream. **(EVELE)**
5. Rocks having large connected holes or pores through which water flows. **(QIEAFUR)**
6. A hot spring where water is forced upward by steam pressure. **(EYEGSR)**
7. Small stream channel often on a steep slope. **(LLIR)**

DOWN

8. The slope of the ground surface. **(EARGDINT)**
9. The act or process of gradual flowing off of water. **(GIARDNAE)**
10. Smaller streams that flow into the main river system. **(ATURTIBRIES)**
11. A flat area bordering a river composed of sediment from the river deposited during floods. **(IAPOLFODLN)** [2 words]
12. These are places where water under pressure reaches the surface. **(SGNRSPI)**
13. A triangular-shaped deposit of alluvial material at the mouth of a river. **(LEDTA)**
14. Large flowing water in a channel over land. **(REVRI)**

SECTION 9

UNDERSTANDING THE PROCESSES AND CYCLES OF WEATHER AND CLIMATE

169. Weather Expressions with Missing Letters

★ The words or phrases below have every second pair of letters missing. Read the clue, then choose the correct missing pairs of letters for each word from the Choice Box. Each pair will be used once.

CLUES

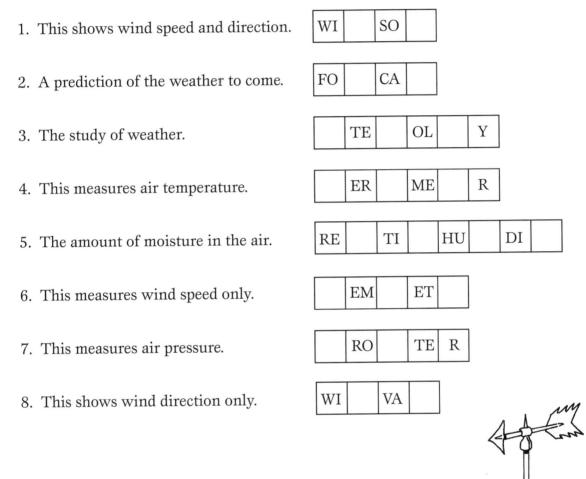

1. This shows wind speed and direction.

| WI | | SO | |

2. A prediction of the weather to come.

| FO | | CA | |

3. The study of weather.

| | TE | | OL | | Y |

4. This measures air temperature.

| | ER | | ME | | R |

5. The amount of moisture in the air.

| RE | | TI | | HU | | DI | |

6. This measures wind speed only.

| | EM | | ET | |

7. This measures air pressure.

| | RO | | TE | R |

8. This shows wind direction only.

| WI | | VA | |

CHOICE BOX

VE	RE	ND	ME	OG	OR
ER	TH	LA	TE	CK	ST
MO	AN	OM	TY	MI	BA
ME	ND	NE			

170. Grouping Climate Vocabulary

★ Choose 2 or 3 words or expressions from the Choice Box that fit each climate study area. Some words can be used more than once and some words may not be used at all.

Area of Study	Words
1. Seasons	
2. Humidity	
3. Deserts	
4. Thermometer	
5. Clouds	
6. Blizzard	
7. Tornado	
8. Hurricane	
9. Monsoon	
10. Precipitation	
11. Thunderstorm	
12. Rainbow	

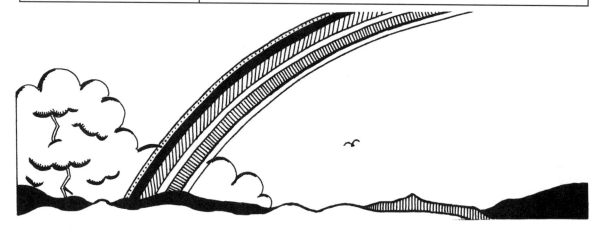

CHOICE BOX

Pot o' Gold, sandy, cold, due to rotation and revolution, water vapor, very little cloud cover, moisture, hot, saturation point, mercury, stratus, destructive, blinding snowfall, has quieter eye, seasonal wind, spiral action, rain, dry, snow, 4 per year, cold heavy snow, affects wide area, lightning, cumulus, thunder, hail, cirrus, common in India, sleet, violent, cumulonimbus

171. Science/English Crossover Weather Grid

★ Below are different English grammar-term headings. You are to use words from the Choice Box that *could* apply to weather conditions and fit under each heading. Each word you choose must begin with the letter on the left. Not all words in the Choice Box will be used. One is done for you to help you get started.

	Nouns	Verbs	Adverbs	Adjectives
W	water			
E				
A				
T				
H				
E				
R				

CHOICE BOX

energize	wild	thundered	tornado	highly
expanding	arid	southerly	hail	reborn
torrentially	tropical	hot	heated	refreshing
wet	running	erratic	ecologically	advanced
rain	westerly	atmospherically	~~water~~	enormous
energy	watered	air	renewed	
easterly	heavily	environment	relatively	

172. How One Weather Item Is <u>Not</u> Like Another

★ Many things in the climate or weather around us have differences, even though they may be connected in some way. Your task is to describe how the two items in each line differ. Resource materials may be required. Be sure to use complete, proper sentences for your answers.

1. Tornado, Hurricane _____
_____

2. Rain, Hail _____
_____

3. Cyclone, Monsoon _____
_____

4. Blizzard, Snow _____
_____

5. Front, Jet Stream _____
_____

6. Wind Sock, Wind Speed _____
_____

7. Downdraft, Updraft _____
_____

8. Lightning, Thunder _____
_____

9. Anemometer, Barometer _____
_____

10. Forecast, Weather Broadcast _____
_____

173. How One Weather Item Is Like Another

★ Many things in the climate or weather around us have similarities, even though at first they may appear to be very different. Your task is to describe how the first item (A) is somehow like the second item (B). Be sure to use complete, proper sentences for your answers.

1. (A) Rain   (B) Snow

_____

_____

2. (A) Sleet   (B) Hail

_____

_____

3. (A) Wind   (B) Breeze

_____

_____

4. (A) Summer heat   (B) Winter cold

_____

_____

5. (A) Wind sock   (B) Wind vane

_____

_____

6. (A) Cloud   (B) Fog

_____

_____

7. (A) Hurricane   (B) Cyclone

_____

_____

8. (A) Thunderstorm   (B) Cloudburst

_____

_____

174. Weather Speculation and Information

★ On line A, describe what you think the word or expression means.

★ On line B, give the dictionary or glossary definition of the word or expression.

1. Meteorologist   (A) _____

                              (B) _____

2. Jet Stream   (A) _____

                              (B) _____

3. Updraft   (A) _____

                              (B) _____

4. Wind Vane   (A) _____

                              (B) _____

5. Isotherm   (A) _____

                              (B) _____

6. Front   (A) _____

                              (B) _____

7. Air Mass   (A) _____

                              (B) _____

8. Air Pressure   (A) _____

                              (B) _____

175. Design a Storm

★ In this unique exercise, you are to design or draw the weather conditions that would exist in an environment during a storm of your choice. Label where necessary.

Storm Types (*circle choice*): Tornado, Hurricane, Cyclone, Blizzard, Thunderstorm

★ Now research the type of storm you have chosen and describe what weather conditions exist at the time the storm is occurring. Write your answer on the back of this sheet.

176. Watch Out for Hail Damage

Let's look at how destructive a hailstorm can be to a farmer. It takes months of work and extensive financial investment to plant, grow, and harvest a crop. Consider the financial implications a hailstorm of a few minutes can have on a farmer's annual income.

★ Your task is to use the information in this chart to calculate the total cost for the amount of acres planted, the potential amount or how much money would have been made, and the amount of money lost by the farmer because of the indicated percent of hail damage.

Crop	Cost of Production per Acre	No. of Acres	Total Cost	Market Price per Bushel	Potential Bushels per Acre	Total Potential Income	% of Damage	Loss from Potential Income
Wheat	$75.00	320		$3.00	30		90%	
Flax	$109.00	640		$7.50	34		92%	
Peas	$82.00	120		$4.25	40		64%	
Soybeans	$91.00	700		$7.42	28		99%	
Oats	$68.25	75		$2.11	51		68%	
Canola	$77.00	1,010		$8.00	39		100%	
Barley	$67.00	327		$2.25	38		64%	
Corn	$75.00	283		$3.50	27		98%	

177. Weather Vocabulary

★ Listed below are two sets of 14 weather-related words. Use all letters *only once per set* to complete the words below.

SET A | A B C D E F G H I J L M N O P R S T U V W X Y Z

1. C __ IMATE

2. __ET STREAM

3. C__ __ LONE

4. DE __ POINT

5. __ ONS __ON

6. PRECI__ITAT__ON

7. __LI__ZARD

8. E__O__PHERE

9. E__APORATE

10. H__R__ICANE

11. __TMOSPHER__

12. __ORECAS__

13. TOR__A__O

14. LIG__TNIN__

SET B | A B C D E F G I L M N O P R S T U V W Y Z

1. TURB__LENCE

2. ISO__AR

3. AERA__ION

4. WESTER__IES

5. ANTI__ __CLO__E

6. A__ID

7. SNO__

8. R__IN

9. __OLDRUM__

10. DO__PLER

11. ENV__RON__ENT

12. E__APORATI__N

13. __RE __ ZIN__ POINT

14. O__ONE

178. Which Weather Pattern Is It?

★ A climate or weather event is hidden in each description. Choose the correct answer from the Choice Box. Not all answers in the Choice Box will be used.

1. A large, destructive, spiral-shaped weather pattern usually formed over the area south and east of Key West, Florida. _____

2. A highly destructive land-based spinning storm that lasts only a short time. _____

3. Precipitation that occurs in colder climates. It arrives in hard pellets during the colder part of the year. _____

4. Precipitation that occurs in colder and warmer regions. It arrives in hard pellets during the warmer seasons. _____

5. Precipitation that occurs in a broad range of climatic conditions and is of particular interest to the agricultural sector of the economy. _____

6. An electrical charge is a dominant forest-fire starter. It was very much in evidence as Mount St. Helens erupted. _____

7. This weather condition is a problem for modern industrialized countries. This is especially true where the humidity is high. _____

8. This weather condition is very evident in Montana but almost never in Florida. _____

CHOICE BOX

snow	thunder	sleet	tsunami	a clear day
lightning	hurricane	tornado	rain	smog
hail	cyclone			

179. Weather Tripod Connections

★ Listed below are 14 sets of three words that all have something in common in the area of weather or climate. Write in the blank space what each set has in common. A Choice Box has been provided. Two of the answers are used twice. Some are not used at all.

1. Tornado	cyclone	hurricane	_____
2. Frost	snow	sleet	_____
3. Water vapor	fog	clouds	_____
4. Stratosphere	exosphere	ionosphere	_____
5. Smog	smoke	car emissions	_____
6. Argon	nitrogen	oxygen	_____
7. Stratiform	cirrus	cumuliform	_____
8. Lightning	thunder	rain	_____
9. Swirling	small area	destruction	_____
10. Predicting	Doppler radar	measuring	_____
11. Dew point	relative humidity	saturation point	_____
12. Westerlies	turbulence	Easterlies	_____
13. Celsius	thermometer	Fahrenheit	_____
14. Breeze	storm	gale	_____

CHOICE BOX

pollution	forecasting	precipitation	storms	wind
sunshine	air	temperature	thunderstorm	chickens
tornado	atmosphere	moisture	Westerlies	fog
freezing	clouds			

180. Climate/Weather Reverse Questions

★ Here is a reversal of sorts. You are given the answers to a series of questions about weather and climate studies. Your task is to make an intelligent question that would be suitable for each answer.

1. The air circulates above the Earth in large convection currents.

   _____

   _____

2. Deserts are regions on Earth that receive less than 25 cm of rainfall in a year.

   _____

   _____

3. The term "climate" actually refers to the average weather patterns over a number of years in an area.

   _____

   _____

4. Relative humidity tells how near the air is to being totally saturated.

   _____

   _____

5. The term "dew point" refers to the temperature at which dew will form on an object outside.

   _____

   _____

6. Clouds are visible particles of water floating in the air.

   _____

   _____

7. Fog is a cloud at ground, or near ground, level.

   _____

   _____

8. A thunderstorm can be created when warm moist air is thrust upwards, cools, and then condenses.

   _____

   _____

181. Climate/Weather Expressions

★ Study the descriptions of the weather-related terms and then choose the correct answer from the Choice Box to fit each description.

1. This is the region of calm weather near the equator feared by early sailors.

2. ____ lines are on a weather map. They join the areas with the same temperature.

3. The name of the zones between the Polar regions and the Tropic Zone.

4. The name of the area or region with yearly rainfall of less than 25 cm.

5. Relative ____ tells how close the air is to its point of saturation.

6. ____ rain is connected to areas of low atmospheric pressure (cyclone).

7. These storms in India are seasonal winds that blow from sea to land part of the year and from land to sea at other times of the year.

8. This was caused by poor farming techniques in the 1930s that turned the soil to dust.

9. These are the boundaries where different masses of air collide.

10. The ____ effect is caused by the trapping of heat coming off a planet's surface.

CHOICE BOX

fronts	monsoons	humidity	cyclonic	isothermal
Dust Bowl	temperate	doldrums	desert	greenhouse

182. It's Windy

★ Use only the letters in the grid to find the words needed to fill in the blanks below. Some letters are used more than once.

Q	B	D	E	M
C	O	U	I	T
F	A	W	R	N
G	Z	S	L	X

1. Most sand grains carried by the wind are made of _____.

2. _____ is the name given to wind erosion of loose material at ground level.

3. During the 1930s, much of the Midwest suffered loss of topsoil from wind erosion. This area was called the "_____ Bowl."

4. _____ is the scrubbing or sandblasting effect of sand grains carried by the wind.

5. The wind is said to be _____ when it is not moving.

6. _____ on "wind farms" produce electricity.

7. Sand _____ are wind deposits in the desert and along coastlines.

8. A _____ is the name given to wind from 4 to 31 mph.

9. A _____ is the name given to wind from 32 to 63 mph.

10. A _____ is the name given to wind from 64 to 75 mph.

183. Atmosphere: Eliminating the Negative and Explaining "Why"

★ This assignment is unusual because you are *not* to choose the correct answer to fit into the space in each sentence. Instead, *you must choose (circle) the least correct answer*. There are three possible answers at the end of each sentence. One is absolutely correct or true, one could be true, and one is false or incorrect. You must explain *why* the answer you circled is completely wrong or incorrect, or how it does not fit the context of the sentence.

1. 78% of air consists of _____. **(oxygen, nitrogen, compressed gases)**

   _____

   _____

2. The Earth's _____ holds the air molecules close to the surface.
   (density, gravity, uniformity)

   _____

   _____

3. Air pressure is measured with a _____.
   (barometer, mercury barometer, mercury thermometer)

   _____

   _____

4. The layer of air nearest the Earth is called the _____.
   (crust, atmosphere, troposphere)

   _____

   _____

5. The strong winds of the tropopause are called the _____.
   (jet stream, jet propulsion, west-to-east stream)

   _____

   _____

6. The thin, almost weather-free area above the troposphere is called the _____.
   (mesosphere, stratosphere, biosphere)

   _____

   _____

7. The atmosphere is heated by the _____ energy of the sun.
   (luminous, radiant, liquid)

   _____

   _____

184. What's the Weather Like Outside?

★ Describe the following weather conditions using at least three one-word statements for each. The first one is completed for you.

Weather Condition	Description
Tornado	dangerous, fast, swirling, frightening
Hurricane	
Rain	
Clouds	
Fog	
Smog	
Sunshine	
Hail	
–40° F	
110° F	
Arid	
Cyclone	
Snow	
Wind	
Overcast	
Thunderstorm	
70° F	

185. Facts About Tornadoes

★   **A. In the blank next to each description in Set 1, write the letter of the related term from Set 2.**

SET 1

_____ 1. Any material caught in the wind

_____ 2. The source of the tornado

_____ 3. The shape of a tornado

_____ 4. The direction of the winds in a tornado in the Northern Hemisphere

_____ 5. The approximate diameter of a tornado

_____ 6. The usual direction a tornado travels

SET 2

a. Funnel

b. Counterclockwise

c. 200 yards (320 m) to 2 miles (3.24 km)

d. Debris

e. Northeast

f. Thunder clouds

★   **B. Read the following statements. If a statement is true, circle T; if false, circle F.**

T   F   1. The safest place in a tornado is in your car with the windows rolled up.

T   F   2. A waterspout is a hurricane over water.

T   F   3. There are more than 710 tornados in the U.S. each year.

T   F   4. The travel speed of a tornado across the ground is approximately 22 mph (35 kph).

T   F   5. The wind speed in a tornado can exceed 210 mph (340 kph).

T   F   6. Normal travel distance for a tornado is 25 miles (40 kilometers) before it dissipates.

T   F   7. Most tornados occur in the middle of the U.S.

T   F   8. The height of the tornado season is winter and early spring.

186. Stormy Hurricane Clues

★ **Let's see how much you know about hurricanes. Place the correct answers to the clues on the left into the answer boxes on the right.**

1. Cool air spins or spirals because of the Earth's _____.

2. The direction of hurricanes in the Southern Hemisphere.

3. The center of a hurricane.

4. The name given to a hurricane in the Western Pacific.

5. The hurricane eye is an area of very low _____.

6. Hurricanes die when they move over _____.

7. This Gulf is a main strike area.

8. The shape of a hurricane.

9. The name given to a hurricane in the Philippines.

10. The name given to a hurricane in Australia.

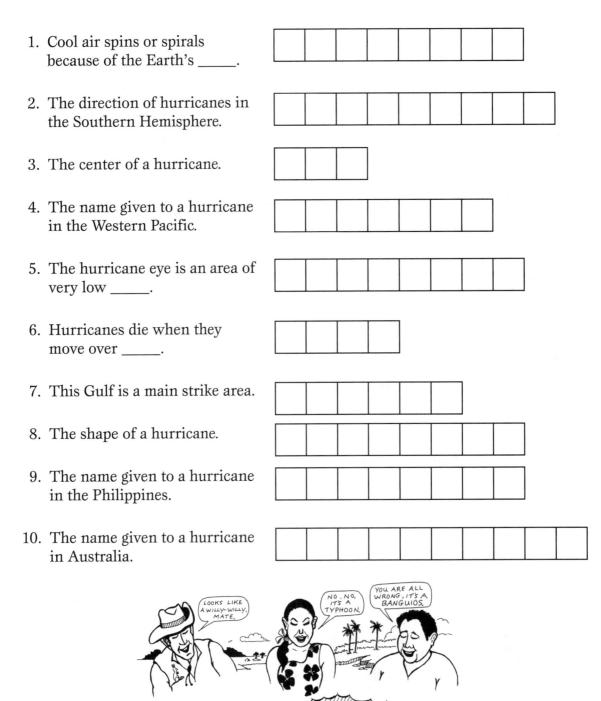

Copyright © 2003 by John Wiley & Sons, Inc.

187. Weather Conditions

★ Listed below are different weather conditions, weather-related events, or concerns. Your task is to pick people from the Choice Box who would be interested in or affected by the condition, event, or concern and explain how it affects them.

1. UV (Ultraviolet) Report: _____

   Why? _____

2. Marine Forecasts: _____

   Why? _____

3. Drought Conditions: _____

   Why? _____

4. International Weather Reports: _____

   Why? _____

5. Microburst (Severe wind blast from thunderstorm): _____

   Why? _____

6. Wind Gusts: _____

   Why? _____

7. Heat Wave: _____

   Why? _____

8. Smog Alert: _____

   Why? _____

CHOICE BOX

campers	military	people with difficulty breathing	sunbathers
sailors	bathers	scuba divers	travelers (vacationers)
gardeners	seniors	people concerned about	joggers
farmers	kite flyers	skin cancer	

188. Atmosphere Expressions

★ Use all the letter pairs in the Choice Box to fill in the answers to the clues about atmosphere expressions.

CLUES

1. 78% of the air is ____.

2. The atmosphere helps ____ the Earth.

3. ____ makes up 21% of our air.

4. The atmosphere has mass and ____.

5. ____ is used to measure air pressure.

6. ____ is the layer of the atmosphere nearest the Earth.

7. ____ is a high level east-to-west wind current.

8. Air is heated by this process.

9. The name of moving air.

10. This dirties the atmosphere.

11. ____ is the mixture of fog and smoke.

12. The ____ of the atmosphere determines its density.

ANSWER GRID

1. | | | T | R | | | |
2. P | R | | | E | |
3. | | Y | G |
4. V | O |
5. B | A | | | M | E | | | R |
6. | | O | P | O | | | H | E | R | E |
7. J | | | | R | E |
8. | | N | V | | | | O | N |
9. W | | | D |
10. P | O | | | U | T | I | | |
11. S | M |
12. T | E | | | E | R | | | U | R | E |

CHOICE BOX

OG	IN	TE	CO	RO
TR	CT	OT	ST	EN
SP	NI	ET	AM	ON
MP	EN	LL	AT	ME
TI	EC	OG	LU	OX

189. The Solstice and Equinox

QUICK ACCESS
information

★ Find the words from the Choice Box that should appear in each numbered space located in the paragraphs. Place the words in the corresponding numbered spaces on the left. No word may be used more than once.

1. _____
2. _____
3. _____
4. _____
5. _____
6. _____
7. _____
8. _____
9. _____
10. _____
11. _____
12. _____
13. _____
14. _____
15. _____
16. _____
17. _____
18. _____
19. _____
20. _____

The term 1 , which literally means "sun 2 ," describes the period of 3 when the sun is either at its 4 northerly point or its most 5 point.

The summer solstice, which occurs on June 22 or 23 6 year, is the time when the sun's 7 is 8 north. This is the 9 day or period of sunlight during the year and the shortest 10 .

The winter solstice, which occurs on 11 22 or 23, is the day the 12 path is farthest 13 . This is the 14 day or period of sunlight during the 15 and the longest night.

The term equinox, which literally means " 16 ," is given to the time when night and day are equal in 17 .

The vernal 18 comes after the winter solstice and occurs on March 21 or 22. The 19 equinox comes after the summer solstice and occurs on September 22 or 23. The equinox days have 20 hours of sunlight and 12 hours of night.

CHOICE BOX

12	each	stops	farthest	path
equal	south	equinox	sun's	longest
southerly	most	year	December	length
shortest	time	autumnal	solstice	night

211

190. The Weather Terms Wordsearch

★ Locate and circle the answers to the clues in the grid. The answers have been provided after the clue; however, they have been scrambled. Study the clue, then decipher the answer.

U	P	D	R	A	F	T	H	U	N	D	E	R	S	T	O	R	M	S	T
B	E	R	M	Y	D	A	T	E	S	O	H	T	R	E	J	O	N	I	N
I	S	O	T	H	E	R	M	S	T	W	C	S	A	T	S	O	T	S	O
H	R	E	O	J	N	S	T	O	A	N	U	T	O	R	N	A	D	O	B
S	A	R	E	G	J	K	H	N	R	D	I	M	K	A	T	H	C	B	R
W	I	E	A	T	Y	M	A	G	E	R	N	I	U	P	W	E	R	A	N
A	R	B	A	V	C	A	I	E	V	A	W	T	S	O	R	N	K	R	A
S	M	R	H	J	L	I	L	R	L	F	O	R	E	C	A	S	T	S	D
T	A	N	P	L	E	R	A	O	F	T	G	R	W	Q	I	A	H	Y	F
O	S	D	E	W	A	B	S	W	E	Z	U	X	T	U	N	K	R	I	R
R	S	J	E	T	S	T	R	E	A	M	B	R	N	A	T	A	S	G	O
E	H	U	R	R	I	C	A	N	E	D	N	A	E	S	R	E	H	G	N
F	U	N	N	E	L	S	M	E	T	E	O	R	O	L	O	G	I	S	T

1. The name of a rising current of air. **(RDPUATF)**

2. The name of the most common type of storm. **(DNUTHEOTSRRM)**

3. A fast-moving ribbon of air high above the Earth. **(TEJMAERTS)**

4. Lines connecting areas of the same atmospheric temperature. **(REHTISOMS)**

5. A violent swirling storm moving over a small area. **(NROTADO)**

6. The name given to weather predictions. **(SACEFORTS)**

7. The shape of a tornado. **(NNFUEL)**

8. This person studies weather. **(ROETMEGOLOIST)**

9. A large body of air with the same moisture pattern. **(AMRAISS)**

10. The place where weather changes occur. **(NORFT)**

11. Lines that connect areas of the same air pressure. **(ABISORS)**

12. The name of a falling air current. **(TNWDODRAF)**

13. A huge, violent storm that develops over the ocean. **(HUNACIRRE)**

14. The name of precipitation. **(IARN)**

15. The name of falling ice in the summer. **(IAHL)**

ANSWER KEY

SECTION 1

1. The Earth: A Real Puzzler

1. Earth
2. processes
3. daily
4. Carson
5. nurture
6. environment
7. pollution
8. reap
9. sow
10. sensitive
11. permafrost
12. scar
13. Northern
14. time
15. complex
16. between
17. resources
18. ecological
19. more
20. better

2. Earth Science Vocabulary

10 crust
5 igneous
9 asteroid
8 equinox
1 atom
7 hydrosphere
2 convection
3 condensation
4 hurricane
6 eclipse

O	A	R	O	O	E	T	E	O	P	R	I	H	M	E
C	O	N	D	E	N	S	A	T	I	O	N	Y	D	Q
B	R	W	O	P	C	R	P	A	G	H	E	D	T	U
W	E	J	U	N	C	R	U	S	T	W	C	R	U	I
A	T	O	M	U	P	W	T	T	J	T	L	O	P	N
H	U	R	R	I	C	A	N	E	T	R	I	S	I	O
I	G	N	E	O	U	S	U	R	B	A	P	P	O	X
I	V	Y	W	P	Q	U	K	O	P	L	S	H	W	G
M	C	O	N	V	E	C	T	I	O	N	E	E	V	H
C	R	U	O	P	W	R	E	D	H	M	T	R	O	O
R	O	M	W	E	T	C	X	Y	L	Y	I	E	W	J

S	O	L	S	T	I	C	E	T	V	W	O	U	T	S
A	T	O	M	I	C	P	A	R	T	I	C	L	E	E
U	E	T	P	R	Y	T	R	E	R	N	E	R	V	D
N	I	W	Y	T	C	Q	U	I	S	D	R	A	T	I
I	U	A	O	P	L	P	T	A	V	E	T	U	E	M
V	R	T	G	M	O	O	N	O	M	W	S	T	U	E
W	A	E	H	J	N	V	A	P	E	R	T	G	S	N
X	L	R	U	B	E	R	U	S	T	R	I	P	A	T
P	K	B	U	L	M	T	R	U	W	E	V	G	H	A
W	P	V	J	K	E	W	B	O	M	E	T	E	O	R
C	O	R	E	B	R	E	K	T	F	A	S	Y	T	Y

3. Mineral Identification

1. color
2. luster
3. heft
4. streak
5. texture
6. fracture
7. cleavage
8. hardness

4. Geoscience Word Completions

SET A

1. RIFT ZONE
2. AXIS
3. TOPOGRAPHY
4. VALLEY
5. GLACIER
6. STACK
7. STALACTITE
8. QUARRY
9. STALAGMITE
10. STRIPMINE
11. SUBDUCTION
12. EROSION
13. PLATE TECTONICS
14. LUSTER
15. WATER TABLE
16. JOINT

SET B

1.	LANDSLIDE	9.	LITHOSPHERE
2.	JET STREAM	10.	LAVA
3.	ORE	11.	INDEX FOSSIL
4.	MINERAL	12.	QUARTZ
5.	MOHO	13.	GEODE
6.	MAGMA	14.	KETTLE LAKE
7.	WIND	15.	IGNEOUS
8.	CARBON	16.	SEDIMENTARY

5. Volcanic "Same As" Vocabulary

Answers will vary. These are suggestions.

1. Lava is magma that has flowed to the surface of the Earth.

2. Aa lava is rough textured, slow flowing, and can contain blocks of material called block lava.

3. Volcanic dust is similar to volcanic cinders because they both can be airborne and both come from volcanic eruption.

4. Volcanic bombs can be similar to war bombs because they both burst on impact.

5. A shield volcano and a composite volcano are both created by volcanic activity.

6. A volcano and an earthquake are both caused by violent action in the Earth's crust.

7. A tsunami and a normal ocean wave both contain energy. Both can be destructive depending on the degree of energy in each.

6. Volcano Expressions with Missing Letters

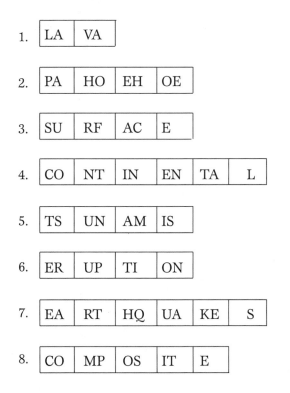

1. | LA | VA |

2. | PA | HO | EH | OE |

3. | SU | RF | AC | E |

4. | CO | NT | IN | EN | TA | L |

5. | TS | UN | AM | IS |

6. | ER | UP | TI | ON |

7. | EA | RT | HQ | UA | KE | S |

8. | CO | MP | OS | IT | E |

7. Researching Famous Geoscientists

Answers will vary. These are suggestions.

Alfred Wegener (Born 1880; Died 1930)
Area of Work/Study: Continental Drift/Plate Tectonics, also Meteorology
Two Life Facts or Contributions:

1. He proposed the theory of Continental Drift now called Plate Tectonics.

2. He pioneered the use of weather balloons to study air circulation.

Isaac Newton (Born 1642; Died 1727)
Area of Work/Study: Study of Motion and Gravity
Two Life Facts or Contributions:

1. He discovered the form of mathematics called calculus.

2. He developed the three basic laws of motion. (He was one of the few true geniuses to have existed.)

James Hutton (Born 1726; Died 1797)
Area of Work/Study: Earth Science
Two Life Facts or Contributions:

1. He developed the concept of the rock cycle, which showed the interrelationship between igneous, sedimentary, and metamorphic rocks.

2. He stated that fossils could be used to study the nature of their original environments.

Johannes Kepler (Born 1571; Died 1630)
Area of Work/Study: Mathematics/Solar System/Optics
Two Life Facts or Contributions:

1. He showed that the planets traveled around the sun in elliptical orbits.

2. He was the first to explain how the human eye works. He is called the "Father of Modern Optics."

8. Earth Science Vocabulary Vowelless Puzzle

S	E	D	I	M	E	N	T	A	R	Y	E	M	E	G
A	B	E	R	M	K	L	F	T	C	M	R	N	P	E
L	U	E	R	U	P	T	O	R	R	L	O	P	I	O
L	T	R	T	L	P	R	S	P	A	N	S	R	C	T
U	T	M	A	G	M	A	S	D	T	D	I	T	E	H
V	E	A	S	M	N	P	I	L	E	D	O	M	N	E
I	G	N	E	O	U	S	L	P	R	I	N	I	T	R
A	V	T	L	P	T	R	L	W	P	K	O	N	E	M
L	R	L	A	V	A	V	B	M	N	E	A	E	R	A
F	R	E	A	B	R	A	D	E	V	P	S	R	W	L
A	V	A	L	A	N	C	H	E	K	P	I	A	L	P
M	E	T	A	M	O	R	P	H	I	C	S	L	S	T

9. Volcanoes: Eliminating the Negative and Explaining "Why"

Listed here are the circled answers. The explanations will vary.

1. telegraph
2. crust
3. Delta
4. waves of the Eclipse
5. hypothesis

10. Fast Changes to the Earth's Surface

1, 2, 3, 4, 5, 6, 7, 8	destruction of forest, loss of animal life
1, 2, 3, 5, 6, 7, 8	loss of crops and income
1, 2, 3, 4, 6, 7, 8	displacement of people, loss of homes
1, 2, 3, 4, 6, 7, 8	massive destruction; possible loss of life
4, 6, 8	burial of skiers, hikers, and so on
5, 8	cracking of soil surface
4, 6, 8	upheavals of land forms
1, 2, 3, 4, 6, 7, 8	disruption of such services as electricity
1, 2, 3, 5, 6, 7, 8	possible contamination of ground water
7	refreshing the landscape for new growth

11. Geoscience "Not the Same As" Vocabulary: Part One

Answers will vary. These are suggestions.

1. Lava is the name given to magma as it reaches the surface of the Earth.
2. Soil can contain minerals, but minerals do not contain soil.
3. A water table is the level of water in all the open spaces in the ground, but an aquifer is a water-filled (porous) layer of rock.
4. Topography describes the physical features of an area and geology is the science of the Earth's crust.
5. A tributary is a stream flowing into a larger stream and a meander is the curved path of a river or stream.
6. A stalactite is a deposit that hangs from the ceiling of a cave and a stalagmite is a deposit that extends up from the floor of a cave, usually beneath a stalactite.
7. A gem is a precious stone and talc is a soft non-precious mineral.
8. Strata refers to layers of sedimentary rock, while bedrock is the solid rock underlying topsoil.
9. Saturation means to contain all material at a temperature level and segregation, in science, refers to the collection of heavy minerals at the bottom of molten rock.
10. Sedimentary rock is formed from fragments or sediments, while igneous rocks are formed when molten material solidifies.

12. Geoscience "Not the Same As" Vocabulary: Part Two

Answers will vary. These are suggestions.

1. A moraine is the deposit left by a melting glacier and talus is the pile of rock debris at the base of a rock formation or cliff.

2. An oasis is a moisture-containing fertile area in a desert and a desert is an area of little precipitation and usually intense heat during the day.

3. A fiord is a narrow opening to the sea, often with steep cliffs, and a bay is a wide opening to a sea or lake.

4. Inertia is the resistance to motion or change in direction, whereas energy is the ability to do work.

5. To erupt usually means a quick violent upheaval, while to erode is a slow, gradual process of decay or decomposition.

6. Luster is the character of light as it is reflected on a mineral, while streak is the color of mineral powder from scratching on a hard surface.

7. Ore refers to the groups of minerals mined for profit, whereas mineral refers to inorganic material with a specific chemical composition.

8. A geyser is a formation that shoots out hot water and steam, whereas a spring is a slower upwelling of groundwater to the surface.

9. A lagoon is an area of shallow salt water connected to the sea, whereas a river is a continuously flowing water formation over land.

10. Latitude refers to the distance north or south from the Earth's equator, whereas longitude refers to the distance west or east of the prime meridian at Greenwich, England.

13. Finding Continental Drift Words and Names from Clues and Scrambles

1. CRUST
2. WEGENER
3. WILSON
4. SPREADING
5. PLATE TECTONICS
6. 2 CM
7. MANTLE
8. SHAPE
9. EARTHQUAKE
10. RICHTER
11. FOCUS
12. CRACKS
13. TSUNAMI
14. BOMBS

14. How One Thing Is Like Another in Rock Study

Answers will vary. These are suggestions.

1. Igneous rocks are like metamorphic rocks because they both contain minerals and both were subjected to heat and pressure.

2. Heat is like pressure because both can have an effect on rock formation. Pressure can cause heat.

3. Basaltic magma and granite magma are alike because both form igneous rocks.

4. Foliated rocks are like non-foliated rocks because both are groupings of metamorphic rocks.

5. Intrusive rocks and extrusive rocks are alike because both are igneous rocks and may be the same material. Extrusive rocks can be intrusive material that has solidified at the Earth's surface.

6. The rock cycle is similar to change because in the cycle process of rock formation, change is continually in progress.

7. The texture of a rock is a direct function of its composition as well as other factors.

8. A volcano and a fault are breaks in the Earth's surface. Volcanoes can occur on the fault lines.

15. Geoscience Tripod Connections

Answers will vary. These are suggestions.

1. rock dating
2. caves
3. hydrology (ground water)
4. volcanoes
5. geologic time periods
6. ocean motions
7. rocks
8. Earth motions
9. Earth portions
10. climatic conditions
11. sand
12. storms
13. evidence of past life
14. water flow

16. Geoscience Newspaper Headlines

Answers will vary.

17. Science Problem-Solving with Brainstorming

Answers will vary.

18. Fossils: Part One

1. qualify
2. prehistoric
3. preserved
4. existed
5. footprint
6. evidence
7. frozen
8. mammoth
9. sap
10. trees
11. captured
12. amber
13. tar pits
14. slowed
15. teeth
16. shells
17. volcanic
18. petrified
19. mold
20. dissolved

19. Fossils: Part Two

1. record
2. preserved
3. body
4. supportive
5. trace
6. footprints
7. find
8. clues
9. warm
10. ancient
11. permafrost
12. climate
13. location
14. elevated
15. mountain
16. water
17. logically
18. bottom
19. no
20. 2%

20. Geoscience Search from Clues

1. lava
2. volcano
3. thermal
4. metamorphic
5. rock cycle
6. large crystals
7. quartz
8. igneous
9. pressure
10. abrade
11. arid
12. buoyancy
13. cleavage
14. cohesion
15. erupt
16. era
17. erosion
18. estuary
19. fracture
20. freezing point
21. exfoliation
22. fold
23. seismograph
24. soluble
25. topography

21. Earthquake and the Earth's Interior Adjectives

Answers will vary.

22. Geoscience Adjectives

Answers will vary.

23. Words and Expressions Associated with Geology

1. volcano
2. crust
3. aquifer
4. Continental Drift
5. delta
6. core
7. dune
8. meander
9. glacier
10. fossil
11. flood plain
12. granite
13. gravity
14. magma
15. lava

24. Geoscience Expressions

1. flowers
2. flare
3. nebula
4. caveman
5. Adam
6. pistons
7. seismometer
8. money
9. Einstein
10. potato
11. igneous
12. Tyrannotops
13. toast
14. crater
15. granite
16. glacier
17. repel
18. ice cream
19. shortitude
20. straight

25. Geoscience Relationships

1. S
2. R
3. O
4. O, R
5. UR
6. R
7. S
8. R
9. R
10. R
11. UR
12. R
13. O
14. R
15. S
16. S
17. R
18. S
19. R
20. S
21. S
22. R
23. R
24. S
25. O
26. UR
27. S
28. R
29. S
30. S
31. R
32. O
33. UR
34. R

26. Interesting Geoscience Vocabulary Clues

These are the words to be filled in.

1. pounds	9. can	17. here	24. car
2. press	10. sun	18. ground	25. bright
3. ants	11. man	19. line	26. arch
4. hard	12. eat	20. in	27. then
5. mine	13. plate	21. bath	28. sat
6. top	14. net	22. buoy	29. Cent
7. ton	15. mount	23. thesis	30. brian
8. graph	16. log		

27. Double-Decker Fossil Fuels

1. population, consumption
2. plants, animals
3. bituminous, anthracite
4. heat, pressure
5. peat, lignite
6. hydrogen, carbon
7. gasoline, kerosene
8. oil, natural gas
9. manufacturing, transportation
10. reducing, recycling

28. A Crusty Puzzle

1. fault
2. Mohorovicic
3. mantle
4. lithosphere
5. volcanic
6. shock
7. thicker
8. igneous
9. age
10. sedimentary

SECTION 2

29. The Scientific Method

1. scientists
2. granted
3. paradigm
4. why
5. blue
6. reflects
7. inquisitive
8. problems
9. theories
10. method
11. flaws
12. data
13. experiments
14. thinking
15. hypothesis
16. work
17. fourth
18. test
19. corrections
20. abandoned

30. Scientific Method Expressions

H	Y	P	O	T	H	E	S	I	S
E	X	P	E	R	I	M	E	N	T
P	R	O	B	L	E	M			
P	R	E	D	I	C	T	I	O	N
E	V	I	D	E	N	C	E		
C	O	N	C	E	P	T			
S	U	P	P	O	R	T			
R	E	V	I	S	E				
V	A	R	I	A	B	L	E	S	
D	I	S	P	R	O	V	E		
P	R	O	C	E	D	U	R	E	S
M	E	A	S	U	R	I	N	G	

31. Scientific Method Expressions from Clues and Scrambles

1. THEORY
2. EXPERIMENT
3. TRUTH
4. ABANDONING
5. PROBLEM
6. WHY
7. HOW
8. DATA
9. PLACEBO
10. RESULTS
11. OBJECTIVE
12. SAME
13. INQUIRE
14. TECHNOLOGY
15. OBSERVATION

32. Science Skill Enhancement

1. observing
2. classifying
3. predicting
4. estimating
5. inferring
6. hypothesizing
7. measuring
8. recording

33. Scientific Method Reverse Questions

Questions will vary. These are suggestions.

1. What is an hypothesis?
2. When are scientists not able to conduct proper experiments?
3. How do scientists verify their hypotheses?
4. How can you prove your hypothesis to be wrong?
5. What is the first thing that a scientist does in the scientific method?
6. What happens if a prediction about the results of an experiment is untrue?
7. What happens if one false result occurs out of a thousand positive-result experiments?
8. What do you seek to do when you design an experiment?

34. Francis Bacon: Hypothesis and Scientific Inquiry

1. pioneer
2. scientific
3. gather
4. open
5. develop
6. educated
7. observing
8. understand
9. data
10. hypothesis
11. experimentation
12. proved
13. law
14. published
15. process
16. refined
17. induction
18. permanent
19. agrees
20. fails

35. A Group Research Project: Part One

Answers will vary.

36. A Group Research Project: Part Two

Answers will vary.

37. A Group Research Project: Part Three

Answers will vary.

38. Safety in the Science Lab: Part One

1. avoid
2. partner
3. clutter
4. contact
5. Make
6. outside
7. no
8. eat
9. hand
10. throw
11. immediately
12. operational

39. Safety in the Science Lab: Part Two

1. authorization
2. directly
3. instructs
4. mishap
5. aprons
6. working
7. care
8. hands
9. touches
10. pouring
11. violently
12. ill

40. Safety in the Science Lab: Part Three

1. freeze
2. winter
3. safer
4. after
5. resistant
6. Watch
7. open
8. heated
9. tongs
10. faulty
11. procedure

41. Safety in the Science Lab: Part Four

1. procedure
2. previous
3. glass
4. scale
5. Glass
6. aware
7. clean
8. mouth
9. bring
10. insert

42. The Great Search for Science "In" Words

1. incandescent
2. inanimate
3. inaccurate
4. inaudible
5. inquire
6. incinerate
7. incision
8. incline
9. incoherence
10. incompatible
11. incongruence
12. inconsequential
13. inconsistent
14. incorrect
15. incubator
16. incurable
17. induce
18. induction
19. industry
20. inertia

43. Researching B.C.E. Scientific Thinkers

1. Hippocrates
2. Aristotle
3. Eratosthenes
4. Eratosthenes
5. Archimedes
6. Aristotle
7. Aristotle
8. Hippocrates
9. Aristotle
10. Hippocrates
11. Archimedes
12. Aristotle

44. Finding Pre-1900 Scientists from Clues and Scrambles

1. HIPPOCRATES
2. ARISTOTLE
3. BACON
4. COPERNICUS
5. GALILEO
6. KEPLER
7. HARVEY
8. NEWTON
9. HALLEY
10. HERSCHEL
11. PASTEUR
12. ROENTGEN

45. Finding Post-1900 People of Science from Clues and Scrambles

1. CURIE
2. EINSTEIN
3. WATSON
4. CARVER
5. BEST & BANTING
6. FLEMING
7. JANSKY
8. AVERY
9. SALK
10. GAGARIN
11. CARSON
12. ARMSTRONG

46. The Hypothesis Concept

1. processes
2. core
3. method
4. dictionary
5. situation
6. make
7. proposed
8. reasoning
9. guess
10. explanation
11. exists
12. become
13. occur
14. clearly
15. collect
16. problem
17. help
18. testing
19. experimentation
20. theory

47. The Science Career Graph: Part One

Answers will vary for 1 and 2. These are suggested answers for 1 and 2.

1. The bars indicate the number of persons (in millions) employed in the fields of science.
2. The field of Math & Logic is not so employable as the field of Biological Science.
3. 30 million
4. Math & Logic

48. The Science Career Graph: Part Two

5. 6.3 million
6. 19.5 million
7. 6 million
8. 9 million
9. 8 million
10. 72 million

49. Think About It

Answers will vary. These are suggestions.

1. This view is incorrect because the world is easily viewed from satellite to be a sphere and not a flat surface.
2. There is no physical evidence to support the fact that Apollo is the sun god, that he has a son, or that any actions from mythology has any effect on the Earth whatsoever.
3. Modern telescopes (technology) prove the sun does not revolve around the Earth and that the moon is in orbit around our Earth.
4. A volcano is caused by stressors in the Earth. It has no life form that would cause it to stop erupting by being satisfied.
5. The average automobile with people in it travels more than 15 miles per hour almost every time a person drives it.
6. There is no objective evidence (other than random chance) that the actions and positioning of the heavenly bodies have an effect on the life processes or fortunes of any human being.

50. A Scientific Method Scramble

1. systematic
2. scientists
3. problems
4. examination
5. investigation
6. research
7. knowledge
8. positive
9. negative
10. studied
11. reasoning
12. hypothesis
13. verification
14. deductive
15. observation

SECTION 3

51. Pioneers of Astronomy, Rocketry, and Space Flight: Part One

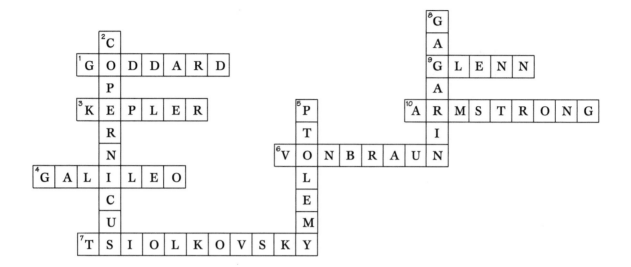

52. Pioneers of Astronomy, Rocketry, and Space Flight: Part Two

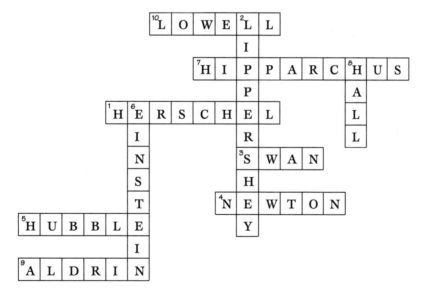

53. Solar System "Things in Common"

Answers will vary. These are suggested answers.

2. People who were rocket pioneers.
3. Things that are associated with Earth.
4. Things that are associated with Earth's moon.
5. Planets that are inner planets.
6. Things associated with Earth's sun.
7. Planets that are outer planets.
8. Things that are associated with Mars.
9. Things that relate to asteroids.
10. Things that are associated with Jupiter.
11. Things that are associated with solar system exploration.
12. People who were early astronomers.

54. Solar System Adjectives

Answers will vary.

55. Solar System Search from Clues

1. Sun	6. Mars	11. comets	16. crater	21. orbit
2. Earth	7. solar flares	12. meteors	17. rotate	22. penumbra
3. Jupiter	8. Mercury	13. centrifugal force	18. sunspots	23. retrograde motion
4. asteroids	9. axis	14. perihelion	19. Moon	24. satellite
5. Saturn	10. Venus	15. photosphere	20. Galileo	25. tides

56. Solar System "Same As" Vocabulary

Answers will vary. These are suggestions.

1. Mars and Earth are both planets with gravity.
2. The sun is similar to the moon in shape. Both are spheres.
3. A comet is similar to a meteor because both are or were traveling in space. Both are influenced by gravitational forces.
4. The umbra is similar to the penumbra because both are shadow forms resulting from an eclipse.
5. Sunspots are related to solar flares because they both emanate from the surface of the sun, and solar flares sometimes occur near sunspot groups.
6. Moon craters are similar to moon maria because both are depressions on the moon's surface.
7. Our moon is similar to phobos because they both revolve around a planetary body.
8. The inner planets are similar to the outer planets because both groups consist of planets that are spheres. Both groups orbit the sun.

57. How One Solar System Object or Event Is <u>Not</u> Like Another

Answers will vary. These are suggestions.

1. A comet is not like an asteroid in the area of appearance. In space a comet appears to be a long, light-reflecting object with a flowing tail, whereas an asteroid is a solid rock piece with no tail or particular reflected brightness.

2. Perihelion is not like aphelion because perihelion is the point in a planet's orbit when it is nearest the sun, and aphelion is the point in a planet's orbit when it is farthest from the sun.

3. Weight differs from mass because weight can change while mass remains constant. The astronaut in outer space has the same mass as he/she did on Earth, but no weight.

4. The photosphere is not like the chromosphere because the photosphere is the visible part of the sun, and chromosphere is the layer of very hot gas around the photosphere of the sun.

5. Longitude is not like latitude because longitude is the measured distance east or west of the prime meridian, and latitude is the measured distance north or south of the Earth's equator.

6. An oblate spheroid is not like a sphere because the oblate spheroid bulges in the center and is flattened on top and bottom, whereas a sphere is an evenly proportioned round object. In a sphere, the center is the same distance from all points at the surface. In an oblate spheroid, the center is at different distances from most points on the surface.

7. An hypothesis is not like a theory because an hypothesis is an educated guess, a proposition, or an assumption based on available information, whereas a theory is a principle founded on a set of facts that have been tested over time.

8. A nebula is not like a nova because a nebula is a large body of gas and dust deep in space, whereas a nova is a star that suddenly increases its energy (light) emissions and then quickly fades in brightness.

9. Rotation is not like revolution because with rotation a body turns or spins on its axis, whereas with revolution a body moves in a path around a central object.

10. Meteors are not like meteoroids because meteors are streaks of light that appear in the sky when a meteoroid enters the atmosphere of the Earth, whereas a meteoroid is a small solid piece of space debris traveling through outer space.

58. Solar System Newspaper Headlines

Answers will vary.

59. Solar System Tripod Connections

1. telescope
2. eclipse
3. space debris or objects
4. planet core
5. sun's surface
6. sunspots
7. inner planets
8. early lunar probes
9. rocket scientists
10. moons
11. comet names
12. outer planets
13. Jupiter
14. Earth

60. Solar System Vocabulary Vowelless Puzzle

A	M	K	L	P	H	O	T	O	S	P	H	E	R	E
P	A	S	T	E	R	O	I	D	N	H	A	M	A	P
H	F	U	G	H	L	P	M	S	D	O	U	S	P	J
E	C	N	E	C	L	I	P	S	E	B	R	D	O	U
L	O	S	V	O	D	F	G	W	M	O	O	F	G	P
I	R	P	E	M	S	M	O	O	N	S	R	V	E	I
O	O	O	N	E	J	A	P	N	T	R	A	D	E	T
N	N	T	U	T	N	R	C	L	S	W	K	E	E	E
L	A	R	S	R	K	S	L	P	U	M	K	I	A	R
M	E	T	E	O	R	M	P	S	N	D	L	M	R	P
L	P	E	R	I	G	E	E	N	B	W	R	O	T	W
C	H	R	O	M	O	S	P	H	E	R	E	S	H	N

61. One Famous Early Scientist Writes to Another

Letters will vary.

62. Solar System Reverse Questions

Answers will vary. These are suggestions.

1. What did Galileo discover about the Milky Way?
2. How does centrifugal force affect a rotating body?
3. What is the shape of the orbits of the planets in our Solar System?
4. Which planet is the mysterious red one?
5. What is the photosphere?
6. What is the difference in temperature between the area of a sunspot and the rest of the sun's surface?
7. What are the four inner planets?
8. Which planet is the largest in our Solar System?

63. Solar System Connections

Answers will vary. These are suggestions.

A *meteorite* is the stone or metallic remains of what once was space debris or small asteroids after they fell to Earth.

The *Earth* is the third planet from the sun in our solar system.

Our sun is part of a group of stars known as yellow main sequence stars.

Jupiter is a planet in our solar system.

Phobos is a moon (satellite) of Mars.

Sunspots are part of the phenomenon that occurs on the surface of the sun.

The *chromosphere* is the hot gas layer surrounding the sun's photosphere, therefore, it is part of the phenomenon that occurs at or near the surface of the sun.

Our Moon is an integral part of the earth/moon interaction (tides) system.

An *eclipse* is part of the phenomenon that results from the positioning of the Earth, sun, and moon.

The *atmosphere* of the planet is part of what is known as the environment of that planet.

Comets are part of the group of heavenly bodies that exist in our solar system and larger universe.

Satellites are part of the group of objects that revolve around planets.

64. One Famous Astronaut Writes to Another

Letters will vary.

65. A Solar System Spiral

R	A	D	³E	C	L	I
G	R	⁸S	A	T	U	P
O	A	E	¹¹A	U	R	⁴S
R	⁷M	N	■	R	N	E
T	E	U	S	O	⁹C	A
E	D	T	I	R	O	S
²R	I	P	X	¹²A	M	O
E	⁶T	E	¹⁰N	T	E	N
T	O	P	S	N	U	⁵S
I	P	U	¹J			

66. Moon Expressions from Clues and Scrambles

1. CRATERS
2. MARIA
3. ECLIPSE
4. METEORITES
5. NEW MOON
6. CRESCENT
7. FIRST QUARTER
8. GIBBOUS
9. SATELLITE
10. ATMOSPHERE
11. SIXTH
12. HIGHLANDS

67. The Solar System Wordsearch

G	A	L	A	X	Y	R	M	I	L	K	Y	W	A	Y	C	R	R	W	A
B	T	A	N	D	E	F	G	H	L	N	M	A	Y	U	M	I	L	P	L
H	P	H	O	T	O	S	P	H	E	R	E	N	J	E	R	W	T	R	P
Y	D	E	T	R	U	E	S	V	B	T	R	I	U	K	E	O	V	G	H
D	M	L	G	S	A	S	D	L	A	F	C	E	P	T	T	Y	E	N	A
R	I	I	R	U	T	Y	E	O	M	V	U	R	I	U	O	P	N	O	C
O	L	U	E	N	Y	G	A	P	N	I	R	P	T	P	O	N	U	P	E
G	J	M	T	S	H	P	R	I	I	P	Y	I	E	N	I	L	S	U	N
E	O	H	W	P	I	L	T	O	P	O	F	A	R	L	O	M	I	L	T
N	T	M	Q	O	M	I	H	P	O	S	B	S	M	N	I	B	M	N	A
E	U	A	U	T	F	V	E	T	C	O	M	E	T	S	C	A	O	P	U
R	W	R	A	S	X	W	A	S	L	S	P	G	M	A	B	D	P	R	R
B	E	S	F	W	A	S	T	E	R	O	I	D	S	D	R	E	I	M	I

1. Galaxy
2. Milky Way
3. Hydrogen, Helium
4. Sunspots
5. Asteroids
6. Comets
7. Alpha Centauri
8. Sun
9. Photosphere
10. Earth, Mars, Mercury, Venus
11. Jupiter

68. Moon Data

1.	C	H	E	E	S	E		
2.	A	L	D	R	I	N		
3.	A	R	M	S	T	R	O	N	G
4.	T	I	D	E	S			
5.	M	A	R	I	A			
6.	H	I	G	H	L	A	N	D	S
7.	C	R	A	T	E	R	S		
8.	V	O	L	C	A	N	I	C	
9.	P	L	A	I	N	S			
10.	M	E	T	E	O	R	S		
11.	L	U	N	A	R			
12.	S	O	L	A	R			

SECTION 4

69. Universe Study: The Early Days

1. astronomy
2. Greek
3. stationary
4. universe
5. geocentric
6. correct
7. Ptolemy
8. planets
9. around
10. stars
11. Copernicus
12. sun
13. Galileo
14. telescope
15. improvement
16. changed
17. study
18. confirmed
19. ridiculed
20. correct

70. Universe Adjectives

Answers will vary.

71. Universe Study Search from Clues

1. weightlessness
2. Zenith
3. spectrum
4. meteorite
5. Solar System
6. galaxy
7. Doppler Effect
8. Light Year
9. constellation
10. gravity
11. star
12. nebula
13. Black Hole
14. astrology
15. magnitude
16. Nova
17. satellite
18. pulsar
19. parsec
20. sidereal period
21. radio telescope
22. ion
23. cosmology
24. binary stars
25. astronomical unit

72. Universe Newspaper Headlines

Answers will vary.

73. Universe Tripod Connections

1. red shift (Doppler effect)
2. Light Year
3. stars
4. constellations
5. early astronomers
6. black hole
7. Retrograde Motion
8. Nova
9. Milky Way
10. Universe
11. relativity
12. parsec
13. orbits
14. ancient astronomers

74. Deeper Universe Vocabulary with Missing Letters

1. | IN | FE | RI | OR |

2. | LU | MI | NO | SI | TY |

3. | VE | LO | CI | TY |

4. | AL | TI | TU | DE |

5. | CO | SM | IC |

6. | DE | NS | IT | Y |

7. | BI | NA | RY |

8. | RE | CE | SS | IO | N |

75. Universe Speculation and Information

Answers will vary.

76. Universe and Solar System Expressions

1. sonar
2. Phobos
3. parsec
4. depth
5. aphelion
6. photosphere
7. astrology
8. white hole
9. Blitzen
10. Newton
11. elastic
12. planet
13. blue dwarf
14. fossil
15. copper
16. horses
17. thermal axis
18. carburetor
19. Saturn
20. highways

77. Comets

1. highly
2. space
3. grab
4. illuminated
5. sun
6. elliptical
7. sections
8. nucleus
9. coma
10. tail
11. several
12. behind
13. directed
14. wind
15. decrease
16. apparent
17. orbit
18. frequently
19. perihelion
20. largest

78. Universe-Study Reverse Questions

Questions will vary. These are suggestions.

1. What is the brightest nebula visible from Earth?
2. What is the Milky Way an example of?
3. What do astronomers look for when they study the universe?
4. What moves in the universe of space?
5. What is a light year?
6. What are Ursa Major and Ursa Minor a part of?
7. What is a star's magnitude?
8. What in our solar system is a yellow, main sequence star?

79. Space-Study Expressions

1. zenith
2. umbra
3. totality
4. supernova
5. sunspot
6. supergiant
7. Jupiter
8. open cluster
9. radio
10. phase

80. Speedy Universe-Knowledge Puzzles

PUZZLE A.

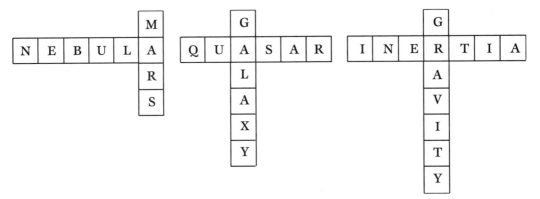

PUZZLE B.
pulsar, star, universe, nova, magnitude

PUZZLE C.
astronomy

81. The Universe Wordsearch

SECTION 5

82. Chemistry Vocabulary

H	Y	D	R	O	G	E	N	D
Y	D	F	U	P	L	O	R	E
S	U	L	P	H	U	R	I	C
O	R	D	E	L	K	R	I	N
U	D	E	R	K	R	E	T	S
R	E	F	G	H	I	L	M	R

hydrogen
PH
sulphuric
sour

C	A	T	A	L	Y	S	T	M
L	A	T	Y	S	T	E	B	K
E	R	C	A	L	T	A	O	O
P	R	O	L	B	E	M	N	L
C	O	M	P	O	U	N	D	S
M	O	P	G	H	I	L	S	M
E	N	E	R	G	Y	E	R	N

catalyst
bonds
compounds
energy

T	A	S	T	E	L	E	S	S
A	R	R	C	E	N	W	E	D
M	O	D	O	R	L	E	S	S
D	E	W	M	N	O	P	R	O
R	E	W	M	N	I	K	L	M
C	O	L	O	R	L	E	S	S
W	R	E	N	L	P	R	O	D

common
tasteless
odorless
colorless

83. Basic Chemical Processes and Substance Expressions from Clues and Scrambles

1. EXPERIMENT
2. COMPOUND
3. CONDENSATION
4. FISSION
5. FUSION
6. ABSORPTION
7. HYDROCARBON
8. NUCLEUS
9. MOLECULE
10. THEORY
11. SOLUTION
12. SUSPENSION

84. What's the Matter, Atom?

Answers will vary.

85. Chemical Elements and Symbols

P	C	A	R	B	O	N	T	R	Y	P	E	R	M
O	K	E	C	A	L	I	R	O	N	C	E	F	H
M	E	D	I	U	V	T	N	E	R	G	L	O	P
D	C	O	P	P	E	R	J	H	R	E	U	P	D
E	R	T	R	W	A	O	X	Y	G	E	N	T	S
W	A	S	B	E	R	G	E	D	R	E	T	V	M
A	Z	U	I	H	E	E	C	R	A	L	C	I	R
N	I	T	N	E	O	N	E	O	M	E	R	T	V
R	O	E	G	L	J	U	T	G	C	A	T	E	R
B	I	T	N	I	D	G	H	E	F	E	R	I	C
V	W	E	R	U	F	Z	I	N	C	D	E	R	M
C	A	L	N	M	E	R	Z	I	T	R	J	O	H
J	O	N	H	T	E	C	F	C	N	S	W	A	T
E	R	B	C	A	R	A	M	K	S	O	N	K	A
E	T	Y	N	S	I	L	V	E	R	T	H	Y	K
J	P	L	E	R	F	C	D	L	R	I	S	A	T
E	P	I	L	T	R	I	E	A	N	T	Y	O	N
M	I	M	E	R	C	U	R	Y	N	A	L	A	S
C	R	U	A	S	T	M	U	E	G	E	N	S	T
G	O	L	D	B	D	R	I	D	E	E	G	V	W

86. Matter and Atom "Not the Same As" Vocabulary

Answers will vary. These are suggestions.

1. Gravity is the attraction or pull of the Earth, whereas grams are a form of measurement of that attraction or pull.

2. Matter is substance, has weight, and occupies space, while a vacuum is the absence of substance in a space.

3. Nucleus is the center of an object, while orbit is the action of a satellite around an object.

4. Protons carry a positive charge in the nucleus, while neutrons are uncharged particles in the nucleus of an atom.

5. An element is a substance or material that cannot be separated into simpler forms of that substance or material, while an atom is the absolute smallest part of an element that can be affected by a chemical reaction.

6. Atomic number is the total number of protons in the nucleus of an atom of an element, while mass number refers to the number of protons and neutrons existing in the nucleus of every atom of a certain element.

7. A periodic table contains listed chemical elements arranged in order of their atomic number, whereas an isotope is any of two or more forms of a specific element that have the exact same atomic number while having different atomic weights.

8. A molecule is a set of atoms joined together by chemical bonds, while a compound is a substance consisting of at least two different chemically joined elements.

9. An acid is a form of matter from which a hydrogen atom can be released in a water solution, whereas a base is a form of matter that reacts with an acid to create a salt.

10. A salt is a chemical substance formed when an acid and a base have a neutralizing effect on each other, whereas an oxide is a chemical compound that has a strong concentration of oxygen.

87. Grouping Chemistry Expressions

1. specific gravity, mass
2. attraction, adhesive force
3. chemical change, release energy
4. change in size, change in shape
5. sugar to alcohol, bacteria
6. neutralizes acid, alkali
7. less than 7 pH, can react violently with metal
8. mix of metals, better use of metals
9. smallest to exist, has properties of element
10. speeds reactions, remains unchanged

88. Chemical Expressions

1. Physical change
2. Chemical property
3. Physical property
4. Chemical bond
5. Chemical change
6. Relative density
7. Chemical reaction

E	R	E	L	A	T	I	V	E	P	H	Y	C	H	E	M	I	C	A	L
C	H	E	M	I	C	A	L	D	S	I	C	H	E	M	I	C	A	L	C
L	E	M	P	R	O	M	B	E	C	A	L	R	A	C	T	I	O	P	H
A	C	H	E	M	R	P	O	N	S	P	H	Y	S	I	C	A	L	R	A
T	P	R	O	L	M	N	N	S	C	H	E	M	I	C	A	L	P	O	N
I	C	E	M	I	C	A	D	I	P	R	C	A	T	O	M	R	R	P	G
P	H	Y	S	I	C	A	L	T	M	E	R	T	I	O	N	E	O	E	E
V	M	A	T	Y	R	T	C	Y	B	R	A	K	W	C	H	A	P	R	M
E	C	H	E	M	O	P	H	C	H	W	E	M	B	O	D	C	E	T	N
C	D	F	R	E	T	D	A	P	R	O	L	M	K	L	W	T	R	Y	O
H	W	E	R	S	U	I	N	C	H	J	K	L	O	P	O	I	T	R	I
Y	B	R	U	S	Y	C	G	P	Y	S	I	C	R	S	E	O	Y	O	N
M	T	U	S	T	R	I	E	P	R	O	L	I	N	S	T	N	C	P	R

89. The A"Maze"ing Atom

1. Matter
2. atom
3. nucleus
4. Protons, neutrons
5. Electrons
6. orbit
7. electrical
8. positive
9. negative
10. no

M	T	B	S	W	E	R	A	S	T	Y	E	L	E	C	G	H	P	R	O
O	A	E	R	T	Z	E	S	K	I	L	O	P	R	E	W	S	E	O	M
N	M	T	T	E	R	A	T	O	M	N	M	U	C	W	U	E	R	T	N
E	B	E	R	T	A	C	A	T	E	O	U	X	R	E	P	R	T	O	R
Y	W	R	E	N	D	A	M	N	W	S	A	C	L	C	E	S	N	S	E
E	L	R	W	F	U	I	P	L	C	E	T	H	R	E	N	B	E	R	T
N	O	R	T	C	E	L	E	S	N	O	R	T	U	M	J	U	I	T	E
S	W	B	I	T	E	L	E	C	T	R	I	C	A	L	P	O	S	I	T
O	R	Y	O	W	R	T	E	C	V	P	R	E	M	G	E	N	E	V	T
M	A	Y	N	A	T	R	E	D	M	R	E	D	A	T	I	V	E	N	O

90. Quick, Learn the Chemical Element

B	S	H	Y	H	C	A	R	B	O	N	C	J	U	Z	G	C	B	N	O
U	I	C	H	Y	O	P	L	M	C	W	E	R	T	I	A	O	S	J	X
T	L	O	E	D	G	O	L	D	A	U	V	E	R	N	S	P	O	U	Y
L	V	W	L	R	H	L	P	M	I	C	W	E	R	C	W	P	D	D	G
E	E	I	I	T	R	A	D	I	U	M	R	A	B	Z	V	E	I	F	E
W	R	L	U	O	F	E	R	R	I	N	W	Z	E	N	O	R	U	E	N
B	A	V	M	N	T	P	O	I	N	C	P	I	R	W	N	C	M	R	O
M	G	E	H	W	N	W	E	R	I	R	O	N	F	E	T	U	N	T	Y
A	T	Y	E	M	N	R	P	O	T	I	C	R	T	Y	M	E	A	Y	P
V	N	I	C	K	E	L	N	I	S	I	L	I	C	O	N	S	I	C	O
S	U	L	F	U	R	S	T	F	G	H	Y	J	U	P	L	N	E	M	N
U	L	M	E	T	B	Y	P	O	W	E	S	T	W	T	Y	U	M	Z	I
M	E	R	C	U	R	Y	H	G	H	Y	D	R	O	G	E	N	H	R	A

Gold   Au   Zinc   Zn
Silver   Ag   Silicon   Si
Iron   Fe   Sulfur   S
Hydrogen   H   Radium   Ra
Copper   Cu   Oxygen   O
Carbon   C   Nickel   Ni
Mercury   Hg   Sodium   Na
Helium   He

91. The Chemical Symbol Wordsearch

E	A	P	b	G	J	A	M	o	X	Z	L	i	A	E	G	L	M	G	A
A	D	G	L	T	Q	X	A	l	y	x	a	Z	A	E	F	Q	R	N	e
R	a	T	K	Z	A	D	E	G	L	P	t	Z	J	L	Z	M	A	E	G
Z	E	D	L	E	M	S	b	T	R	T	V	Z	S	Y	A	u	D	N	i
D	G	L	T	R	n	M	Q	T	V	A	r	Z	T	A	D	G	J	L	N
B	r	Q	L	M	Y	T	S	n	Z	A	Y	D	R	E	G	J	T	V	n
W	X	T	i	T	Y	G	D	B	M	U	T	P	u	A	L	M	H	e	T
T	Z	T	J	C	d	j	N	a	Q	E	M	T	T	Q	O	Z	T	A	H
M	g	g	j	n	E	D	L	D	K	r	T	C	l	Z	G	L	P	T	Z
L	B	T	V	Z	Y	A	M	n	Z	D	T	E	A	g	T	I	T	F	e
S	i	Z	C	a	Z	T	D	E	X	H	g	R	T	Z	A	A	Z	A	Z
A	E	V	Z	D	A	M	C	r	M	Z	Z	Z	A	C	o	D	A	D	T
E	s	M	Q	T	Z	Y	T	Q	Z	n	D	C	T	M	E	Z	L	C	u

Aluminum Al
Antimony Sb
Argon Ar
Boron B
Bromine Br
Cadmium Cd
Calcium Ca
Carbon C
Chlorine Cl
Chromium Cr
Cobalt Co
Copper Cu

Einsteinium Es
Fluorine F
Gold Au
Helium He
Hydrogen H
Iodine I
Iron Fe
Krypton Kr
Lead Pb
Lithium Li
Magnesium Mg

Manganese Mn
Mercury Hg
Molybdenum Mo
Neon Ne
Nickel Ni
Nitrogen N
Oxygen O
Phosphorus P
Platinum Pt
Plutonium Pu
Potassium K

Radium Ra
Radon Rn
Silicon Si
Silver Ag
Sodium Na
Sulfur S
Tin Sn
Titanium Ti
Tungsten W
Uranium U
Zinc Zn

SECTION 6

92. Physical States of Matter

1. circumstances
2. substances
3. solid
4. liquid
5. gas
6. phase
7. observe
8. cohesion
9. molecules
10. atoms
11. force
12. dense
13. shape
14. lesser
15. remain
16. liquid
17. move
18. shape
19. minimal
20. container

93. Standardization of Power

1. INVENTOR
2. CENTURY
3. MEASUREMENT
4. POWER
5. DISCOVERED
6. DRAFT
7. HORSE
8. PULL
9. FEET
10. MINUTE
11. KNOWN
12. HORSEPOWER

94. Double-Sided Antonyms for Relative Conditions of Matter

1. constant
2. condensation
3. dry
4. cold
5. strong
6. sparse
7. light
8. useless
9. vacuum
10. transparent
11. absolute
12. empty
13. stillness
14. light
15. shiny
16. new
17. small

95. Five Processes that Change the State of Matter

Answers will vary. These are suggestions.

1. Melting is the change of a solid to a liquid, whereas freezing is the changing of a liquid to a solid.

2. Melting is the change of a solid to a liquid, whereas evaporation is the change of a liquid to a gas.

3. Freezing is the change of a liquid to a solid, whereas evaporation is the change of a liquid to a gas.

4. Freezing is the change of a liquid to a solid, whereas condensation is the change of a gas to a liquid.

5. Evaporation is the change of a liquid to a gas, whereas sublimation is the direct change from a solid to a gas without passing through an intermediate liquid state.

6. Melting is the change of a solid to a liquid, whereas sublimation is the direct change from a solid to a gas without passing through the intermediate liquid state.

7. Freezing is the change of a liquid to a solid, whereas sublimation is the direct change from a solid to a gas without passing through the intermediate liquid state.

8. Condensation is the change of a gas to a liquid usually by compressing the gas, whereas evaporation is the change of a liquid to a gas.

9. Condensation is the change of a gas to a liquid usually by compressing the gas, whereas melting is the change of a solid to a liquid.

10. Sublimation is the direct change from a solid to a gas without passing through the intermediate liquid state, whereas condensation is the change of a gas to a liquid usually by compressing the gas.

96. A Physical Properties Puzzler

1. mass
2. solid
3. gas
4. shape
5. volume

6. weight
7. color
8. density
9. malleability
10. liquid

97. What Do You Know About Energy?

1. FUELS
2. WORK
3. BODY
4. CHEMICAL
5. WATER

6. GEOTHERMAL
7. SOLAR
8. ELECTRICAL
9. RENEWABLE
10. NONRENEWABLE

98. Particle Theory of Matter

A	C	V	E	R	T	V	C	D	C	E	F	Q	U	T	R	I	M	K	M
P	T	M	I	N	D	S	T	R	O	N	G	E	R	L	O	P	E	S	O
L	D	A	N	I	P	T	A	S	N	V	G	H	T	I	K	A	R	D	V
A	T	T	R	A	C	T	E	D	T	E	W	R	T	C	A	M	C	E	E
S	F	T	T	R	I	C	T	E	I	D	E	N	T	I	C	A	L	S	M
P	O	E	A	E	R	T	Y	E	N	O	P	K	I	M	O	P	O	M	E
E	P	R	T	A	W	W	E	R	U	L	P	O	N	J	N	I	S	N	N
R	J	W	D	E	A	C	L	E	O	G	H	T	Y	O	S	L	E	T	T
T	O	E	R	R	I	L	M	A	U	K	A	Z	V	P	I	J	R	O	P
S	T	M	A	S	P	A	C	E	S	M	A	L	L	Q	S	K	E	B	I
U	R	K	M	G	H	R	V	G	B	I	J	O	N	U	T	L	C	R	R
V	W	E	I	T	Y	G	P	U	R	H	K	R	T	I	S	A	M	E	T
W	A	R	E	T	Y	E	T	A	N	O	T	H	E	R	R	P	I	D	E

1. matter, consists, small, tiny
2. same, identical
3. attracted, another, stronger, closer
4. large, spaces
5. continuous movement

99. Matter: Eliminating the Negative and Explaining "Why"

Listed here are the circled answers. The explanations will vary.

1. vacuum
2. direction
3. theory
4. negative
5. intelligence
6. fossils
7. fixtures

100. Physical Science Newspaper Headlines: Part One

Answers will vary.

101. Physical Science Newspaper Headlines: Part Two

Answers will vary.

102. "Heated" Vocabulary

1	2	3	4	5	6	7	8	9	10	11	12	13	14	15	16	17	18	19
					G	E	O	T	H	E	R	M	A	L				
					A			H										
					S		H	E	A	T								
								R										
								M										
							S	O	L	A	R							
								C										
							C	O	L	D								
								U										
			M		T	E	M	P	E	R	A	T	U	R	E			
			E					L							X			
C	O	O	L			F	R	E	E	Z	E				P			
			T			R									A			
			I			O									N			
			N			Z	E	R	O			C	E	L	S	I	U	S
			G			E									I			O
						E	N	E	R	G	Y				O			L
															N			I
																		D

103. Turn Up the Heat

Grid 1:
```
T H E R M
T H E R O
C E V M C
O X O O O
N P L G U
T A U R P
R N M A L
A S E P E
C I T H V
T O N X P
I O N E I
```

Grid 2:
```
C G A L I
E C N B L
L L I T E
S I A Y O
I N F S T
U I R M O
S C O X C
T A Z N T
H L E M T
E B N I A
R M O S T
```

Grid 3:
```
H E A T M
T M J O E
I P H V L
B V C O T
P I O M I
E P L R N
V S D B G
A D I C E
P W S N T
O X D O X
R A T I S
```

104. Powerful Forces

1. friction
2. gravity
3. electrostatic
4. centrifugal
5. buoyancy
6. magnetism
7. load
8. inertia
9. stress
10. electromotive

105. The Difference Between Mass, Volume, and Weight

1. material
2. object
3. size
4. mass
5. constant
6. expands
7. same
8. different
9. volume
10. gravitational
11. weight
12. location
13. space
14. accumulated
15. blast
16. escaped
17. force
18. Earth's
19. float
20. changed

106. The Mechanical Advantage of a Lever

1. ratio
2. resistance
3. force
4. receive
5. machine
6. enables
7. not
8. fulcrum
9. downward
10. distance
11. apply
12. C
13. upward
14. farther
15. A
16. moves
17. weight
18. increasing
19. equal
20. different

107. What Does That Tool Do?

Answers will vary. These are suggestions.

Tool or Machine	Main Function	Secondary or Other Function
Shovel	digging	lifting, smoothening, chipping, mixing
Wheelbarrow	hauling	mixing bin, storage, transportation
Leash	animal control	barrier, jump rope, belt, tying things
Hammer	driving nails	prying, making holes, gavel, flattening materials, moving stuck objects
Saw	cutting	musical instrument, folk art paint surface
Power drill	drilling holes	sander, power screwdriver
Blender	mixing foods	chopping ice
Tweezers	grasping small objects	plucking, holding, reaching
Pen	writing	drawing, pointing, emergency medical use—tube for tracheotomy
Axe	chopping	hammer, sharpening pegs, lumberjack competition, skinning
Fly swatter	killing flies	fan, decorations—used in commercial ads
Pry bar	lifting	hammer, propping up door, hooking objects, chipping ice

108. Sound "Not the Same As" Vocabulary

Answers will vary. These are suggestions.

1. A sound wave is dependent on the density of the atmosphere it occurs in, whereas a water wave is dependent on the water environment it occurs in.
2. Compression in sound study is a region of crowded air particles, whereas rarefaction is a region of less crowded air particles.
3. Transmitted is a process in which sound waves are sent through matter, whereas an echo is the repeating of a sound by virtue of bouncing or reflecting sound waves off a surface.
4. Absorbed means sound waves have been trapped by a substance, whereas reflected means sound waves have been bounced off a surface.
5. A decibel is a measure of the loudness of sounds, whereas energy is the ability to do work.
6. Amplitude describes the range (scope and extent) of sound, whereas noise is a general term describing certain sounds, usually annoying.
7. Sonar is used in water to locate objects, whereas radar is used in the atmosphere or space to detect objects.
8. Mach number is the scale used to compare the speed of objects to the speed of sound, whereas ultrasonic designates the frequency of mechanical vibrations above the range audible to the human ear.
9. Vibration is the rapid back-and-forth movement of air that can create sound, whereas wave length is the distance between the crest of one sound wave and the crest of the sound wave beside it.
10. Frequency describes the number of sound waves that pass a specific spot, whereas pitch is how high or low a sound is as a function of the vibrations of sound waves.

109. Sounds to Be True

1. waves
2. transmitted
3. absorbed
4. reflected
5. frequency
6. wavelength
7. pitch
8. compression
9. hertz
10. energy
11. noise
12. supersonic
13. amplitude
14. decibels
15. sonar

110. Light "Not the Same As" Vocabulary

Answers will vary. These are suggestions.

1. Absorbed means to take in, whereas reflected means to throw back or bounce back.
2. A mirror is designed to reflect back an image, whereas glass is designed to be seen through.
3. Infrared waves are longer than those of light but not as long as microwaves, whereas ultraviolet waves are not as long as those of light but are longer than x-rays.
4. A vacuum is defined as a space with nothing in it, whereas the atmosphere (of Earth) is the layer of gases immediately above the Earth's surface.
5. Transmitted means to send out, whereas received means to accept in.
6. Transparent means to be able to see clearly through, whereas translucent means there is only partial visibility through an object.
7. Clear means to have no restrictions in terms of vision, whereas opaque means to not be able to see through clearly—not transparent.

8. A prism is a solid figure used to disperse light into the spectrum, whereas the spectrum is a series of colored bars or bands that are dispersed by a prism. The arrangement of the colors is relative to their wavelengths.

9. Frequency describes how often something occurs, whereas hertz is a unit of frequency. Hertz is the number of cycles a vibrating or pulsating event occurs in one second.

10. Concave describes a lens that appears to be caved in or like the inside of a basketball viewed from the center of the ball, while convex describes a lens that is curved outward like the surface of a basketball as you hold it.

111. Physical Science Vocabulary Vowelless Puzzle

V	I	S	C	O	S	I	T	Y	M	R	G	D	M	T
E	R	T	C	E	L	S	I	U	S	G	R	E	O	B
L	I	G	H	T	W	E	I	G	H	T	A	N	L	N
O	A	A	D	H	E	S	I	O	N	K	V	S	E	P
C	T	I	N	E	R	T	I	A	B	I	I	I	C	R
I	O	M	K	P	L	T	D	G	H	N	T	T	U	D
T	M	A	S	S	V	R	C	B	N	E	Y	Y	L	N
Y	R	F	R	I	C	T	I	O	N	T	R	I	E	J
D	R	W	R	T	M	W	L	P	R	I	F	O	T	K
C	A	L	O	R	I	E	G	H	T	C	C	N	R	L
W	A	V	E	W	R	P	D	E	N	E	R	G	Y	M
C	O	N	D	U	C	T	O	R	W	O	R	K	P	N

112. How One Thing Is Like Another in Physical Science

Answers will vary. These are suggestions.

1. Energy is like work because energy is defined as the ability to do work.

2. Adhesion is like cohesion because both mean to stick together or the ability to stick two or more things together.

3. Alternating current is like direct current because both are forms of electrical current.

4. Amplitude modulation is like frequency modulation because both are variations of the transmitting radio wave relative to the signal used, transmitted, or broadcast.

5. Gravity is like magnetism because both can be forces of attraction.

6. Momentum is like centrifugal force because both are forces that can propel an object in a specific direction.

7. Friction is like inertia because both are a form of resistance to motion or change of direction.

8. An atom is like a molecule because an atom is the smallest part of a chemical element that will display the traits of that element, and a molecule is the smallest part of a substance that will display the traits of that substance.

113. Physical Science Tripod Connections

Answers will vary. These are suggestions.

1. gas
2. heat
3. electricity
4. forces
5. sound
6. atom
7. metric system
8. measuring devices
9. magnetism
10. music
11. radiation
12. light
13. reflection
14. speed

114. Physical Science Problem-Solving with Brainstorming

Answers will vary.

115. Unusual Physical Science (Physics) Problems

Answers will vary.

116. Physical Science Search from Clues

1. energy
2. fluid
3. gravity
4. friction
5. heat
6. inertia
7. Kelvin
8. adhesion
9. absorption
10. amplitude modulation
11. chemical energy
12. Brownian motion
13. efficiency
14. molecule
15. weight
16. surface tension
17. mass number
18. mechanics
19. dynamics
20. Absolute Zero
21. stress
22. velocity
23. load
24. mass
25. capillary action

117. Physical Science Words and Expressions

1. ray
2. inertia
3. ion
4. kinematics
5. dynamics
6. hydraulics
7. machines
8. lever
9. pulley
10. equilibrium
11. statics
12. power
13. conduction
14. entropy
15. velocity

118. Double-Sided Physical Science Synonyms

```
M P A R T B R O M W S C K      S C O M P O N E N T E R M
A R F A T O M I C A U O I      U R P N U C L E A R X E O
T O O E X C E L A O B M N      B A O S U R P A S S C L T
T D R F U S E D M R S P E      S T W J O I N E P R H A I
E W C R I D W R O E T A T      T W E D E R M W A E A T O
R M E A D E L E L S I R I      A D R L M O P C R A N I N
F C O N V E R T E P T A C      N C H A N G E A T C G V O
I G N I T E N J C O U T D      C O M B U S T R I T E E P
D F I S S I O N U N T I O      E S P L I T R A C I L V M
E N E R G Y C R L S I V E      W O R K R S Y O L O M O Y
M A I N T A I N E U E O E W    C O N S E R V E E N E R T
T H E R M A L R E D N M K      H E A T R E T E M K A R E
D R U W R I N C R E A S E      R A T G H G A I N K I L R
```

1. work
2. motion
3. part
4. heat
5. power
6. comparative
7. surpass
8. substitution
9. change
10. ignite
11. response
12. split
13. join
14. maintain
15. substance
16. increase
17. atomic
18. particle

119. A Properties of Matter Puzzler

1. compression
2. tension
3. strength
4. cost
5. appearance
6. odor
7. load
8. fatigue

120. Energy, Work, and Power

1. velocity
2. thermal
3. radiant
4. sound
5. conservation
6. nuclear
7. work
8. kinetic
9. temperature
10. chemical
11. created
12. destroyed

121. Mr. Newton and His Laws of Motion

1. motion
2. developed
3. genius
4. Newton's
5. object
6. rest
7. acted
8. sitting
9. kick
10. stop
11. outside
12. second
13. upon
14. rate
15. momentum
16. inertia
17. resist
18. third
19. equal (or opposite)
20. opposite (or equal)

122. Friction Grids

R	E	D	T	B	A	M	T	A
E	S	D	E	R	E	S	B	T
S	N	O	L	U	M	W	E	M
I	B	R	A	K	E	T	R	O
S	T	O	P	P	I	N	G	S
T	P	U	R	O	U	B	E	P
A	L	G	E	A	G	I	N	H
N	N	H	E	L	E	J	E	E
C	A	R	R	I	E	S	R	R
E	O	H	N	S	T	O	A	E
W	A	T	A	N	H	Y	T	B
T	E	B	R	E	G	M	E	R
A	N	C	A	F	O	R	C	E

J	O	I	N	T	S	A	L	L
C	A	T	R	E	J	O	U	I
N	T	S	O	N	E	H	B	Q
T	I	E	A	C	A	R	R	U
R	A	L	R	B	W	E	I	I
E	N	C	A	R	T	I	C	D
S	D	R	N	V	C	L	A	S
K	G	A	O	A	R	E	N	X
H	E	L	T	H	E	A	T	W
T	R	A	O	T	A	W	R	E
A	O	J	E	G	E	G	F	A
W	G	Q	U	I	C	K	E	R
A	S	T	N	O	K	S	R	I

1. force
2. resistance
3. heat
4. quicker
5. liquids

6. stopping
7. generate
8. joints
9. all
10. rough

11. brake
12. lubricant
13. atmosphere
14. wear
15. carries

SECTION 7

123. A Cell Puzzler

1. Tissue
2. nucleus
3. Genes
4. Chromosomes
5. Vacuoles
6. Chloroplasts
7. Mitosis
8. membrane
9. wall
10. Cytoplasm

124. Match the Cells

(5) chromosomes
(7) organism
(2) cell wall
(3) vacuoles
(8) chlorophyll
(9) mitosis
(6) genes
(1) cell membrane
(10) nuclear membrane
(4) cytoplasm

125. Animal and Plant Cell Differences and Similarities

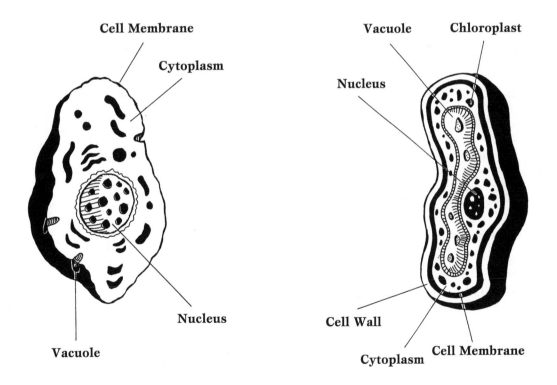

126. Unscramble the Living Matter Words

P	C	Y	T	O	P	L	A	S	M	T	N	U	C	L	E	U	S	X	C
B	O	R	N	E	C	T	R	I	V	E	R	W	U	T	R	A	Q	U	E
P	R	C	H	L	O	R	O	P	L	A	S	T	J	U	P	I	R	M	L
R	W	G	I	D	F	G	H	I	K	L	E	R	T	P	U	I	I	M	L
O	A	E	D	C	H	L	O	R	O	P	H	Y	L	L	P	R	B	O	M
T	S	N	E	M	I	P	R	E	R	D	G	J	M	A	L	N	O	V	E
E	T	E	R	D	R	I	G	V	E	W	I	H	T	S	K	O	S	I	M
I	O	S	S	F	E	D	A	P	F	A	T	S	D	T	E	L	O	L	B
N	J	V	T	N	D	E	N	W	E	T	C	R	E	I	R	E	M	A	R
S	O	C	U	R	O	S	D	E	R	E	W	Q	U	D	T	W	E	R	A
H	T	I	S	S	U	E	C	H	A	R	E	W	A	S	Y	I	S	T	N
N	O	S	T	N	W	A	Y	R	E	T	Y	S	E	R	T	N	U	I	E
C	A	R	B	O	H	Y	D	R	A	T	E	S	Y	S	T	E	M	M	R

1. cytoplasm
2. carbohydrates
3. nucleus
4. chloroplast
5. chlorophyll
6. tissue
7. system
8. fats
9. proteins
10. cell membrane
11. genes
12. ribosomes
13. plastids
14. organ
15. water

127. What Is It? Knowing Reproductive Processes from Clues

1. LIVING
2. FISSION
3. EGG
4. SPERM
5. ZYGOTE
6. FERTILIZATION
7. EMBRYO
8. INHERITED
9. DOMINANT
10. RECESSIVE

128. Grouping Life Science Vocabulary

1. frog, salamander, newt

2. tundra, deciduous forest, grassland

3. hawk, sparrow, crow

4. vacuoles, genes, nucleus

5. weather, rain, storms

6. adaptation, phototropism, biological clock

7. salmon, carp, trout

8. sleep, slow body activity, stored fat

9. grasshopper, ant, butterfly

10. baboon, gorilla, gibbon

11. mimicry, camouflage, disguise

12. iguana, crocodile, alligator

13. rat, mouse, squirrel

14. canines, molars, incisors

15. growth rings, bark, oak

129. Life Science Vocabulary Relationships

E	N	V	I	R	O	N	M	E	N	T	B	B	X	L
O	P	N	I	M	U	B	A	W	P	R	O	T	N	I
B	A	C	T	E	R	I	A	I	P	E	N	O	M	G
N	O	P	I	C	D	A	S	W	M	E	S	V	A	H
A	Q	U	S	X	T	R	U	W	R	S	T	I	U	T
M	U	T	S	A	R	W	D	W	X	C	T	R	A	R
R	T	Y	U	A	I	K	L	O	P	M	R	U	S	E
S	D	A	E	T	R	A	P	M	I	T	O	S	I	S
M	A	S	J	H	K	L	M	O	P	N	R	T	A	P
C	O	N	T	R	O	L	C	E	N	T	E	R	I	O
E	A	R	L	Y	O	R	G	A	N	I	S	M	O	N
Y	A	R	T	R	V	B	R	P	I	L	O	E	V	S
C	H	L	O	R	O	P	L	A	S	T	I	P	L	E

C	E	L	L	D	I	V	I	S	I	O	N	D	E	R
P	H	O	T	O	T	R	O	P	I	S	M	I	P	E
N	F	K	L	O	P	E	R	W	T	F	U	S	K	D
U	M	B	L	P	E	R	T	R	U	C	S	E	E	F
C	H	L	O	R	O	P	H	Y	L	L	C	A	R	G
L	O	P	T	O	M	K	L	O	P	E	L	S	M	H
E	A	T	D	T	D	E	N	R	T	R	E	E	L	I
U	T	E	R	I	N	G	S	U	R	T	M	N	W	L
S	A	R	T	S	N	O	P	Q	E	R	B	N	O	M
A	D	A	P	T	A	T	I	O	N	I	R	P	I	N
M	A	E	R	S	T	E	B	T	J	U	Y	W	T	A
V	G	H	T	E	R	A	I	N	E	T	O	E	Y	S
R	Y	T	O	P	M	K	O	I	L	M	R	W	O	T

Trees 3	Bacteria 4
Mitosis 5	Control center 2
Environment 6	Light response 1
Chloroplast 7	Tissue 9
Virus 8	Early organism 10

130. Find the Endocrine System Pairs

1. control	6. thyroid
2. rate	7. parathyroid
3. glands	8. pancreas
4. hormones	9. adrenalin
5. pituitary	10. reproductive

131. Speedy Cell-Knowledge Puzzles

PUZZLE A

1. nucleus
2. cell
3. virus
4. chromosomes
5. gene
6. cytoplasm
7. chloroplast
8. cell membrane

PUZZLE B

CELL WALL   MEMBRANE   VACUOLES   ORGANISM

PUZZLE C

1. egg
2. pollen
3. mitosis
4. epidermis
5. cloning

132. Life Science from Definitions and Context

1. phototropism
2. dendrochronology
3. biosphere
4. hibernation
5. fertile
6. grassland
7. instinct
8. mimicry

133. Watch Out for Food Poisoning

1. botulism
2. salmonellosis
3. staphylococcal
4. bacteria
5. skin
6. toxins
7. anaerobic
8. warm

134. Basic Plant-World Expressions from Clues and Scrambles

1. DENDROCHRONOLOGY
2. SPORE
3. STAMEN
4. STIGMA
5. TUBERS
6. TRANSPIRATION
7. POLLINATION
8. PHOTOSYNTHESIS
9. OSMOSIS
10. BULB
11. GEOTROPISM
12. PHOTOTROPISM

135. Microorganism Expressions from Clues and Scrambles

1. MICROBIOLOGIST
2. FLAGELLA
3. COLONY
4. VIRUSES
5. ALGAE
6. SINGLE
7. SALMONELLA
8. PROTOZOA
9. CHAIN
10. SPORE
11. BOILING
12. STERILE
13. CLEAN

Fear of microbes or bacteria: BACILLOPHOBIA.

136. The Microorganism and Food Spiral

	¹P	O	I	S	O
T	⁶O	X	Y	G	N
A	E	D	¹¹P	E	O
E	N	■	A	N	U
⁵H	N	S	S	⁷M	S
N	A	T	T	O	²B
O	¹⁰C	N	E	I	O
I	G	A	U	S	T
T	N	N	R	T	U
A	I	I	I	U	L
T	Z	M	Z	R	I
N	E	A	A	E	S
E	E	T	T	⁸A	M
M	R	N	I	D	³S
R	⁹F	O	O	D	A
E	S	¹²C	N	I	L
⁴F	E	V	I	T	M
A	L	L	E	N	O

137. Life Science Controversies: Part One

Answers will vary.

138. Life Science Controversies: Part Two

Answers will vary.

139. Nervous System and Endocrine "Not the Same As" Vocabulary

Answers will vary. These are suggestions.

1. The central nervous system consists of the brain and spinal cord, whereas the peripheral nervous system consists of the nerves that extend out from the brain and spinal cord to the rest of the body.

2. Voluntary responses are those a person has some degree of control over, whereas a person normally cannot consciously control the involuntary system.

3. Sensory nerve cells are those that react to internal or external stimulation, whereas motor nerve cells are those that transmit data from the central nervous system to different parts of the body.

4. Reflex is an automatic response, whereas a learned response is not automatic but must be learned or developed.

5. The brain is located in the skull and is the stimulus/response nerve center, whereas the spinal cord is mostly located in the back and is a major conduit of stimuli and responses.

6. The cerebellum area of the brain controls body balance and muscle coordination, whereas the cerebrum is the area of the brain that controls thinking and reasoning.

7. Paralysis is the lack of movement or the inability to have motor control in an area of the body or the inability to possess movement.

8. The pancreas is an area where a hormone (insulin) is produced, whereas hormones are substances produced in one area of the body and then travel to another part of the body where they do their work.

9. Dwarfism is the result of some process causing shortening of physical stature in a person, whereas giantism is the result of some process causing lengthening of physical stature of a person.

10. The adrenal glands secrete the hormone adrenalin and are located near the kidneys in the human body, whereas the thyroid gland secretes a growth hormone and is located near the trachea in the human body.

140. Life Organisms: Eliminating the Negative and Explaining "Why"

Listed here are the circled answers. The explanations will vary.

1. microscope
2. antibodies
3. environmental
4. mitosis
5. marketing process
6. polluted
7. run
8. phototropism

141. Life Sciences Speculation and Information: Part One

Answers will vary.

142. Life Sciences Speculation and Information: Part Two

Answers will vary.

143. All About the Biosphere/Biome

1. organisms
2. environment
3. multiply
4. types
5. adapting
6. surroundings
7. elements
8. food
9. air
10. climate
11. conditions
12. surface
13. region
14. biosphere
15. survival
16. distributed
17. plants
18. biomes
19. safe
20. needs

144. The Biome, or Life Zone: Part One

Tundra: snow, cold, short summer, lemmings, musk ox, snowy owl

The Taiga (Swamp Forest): water, conifers, elk, moose, lumber resource, largest biome

The Deciduous Forest: four distinct seasons, raccoons, thick forest floor, trees shed leaves in fall, south of taiga, has broad leaves

145. The Biome, or Life Zone: Part Two

The Desert: cactus, largest in Sahara, dry, snakes, hot by day, cold at night, lizards, sagebrush, quick evaporation

The Grassland: called prairie, tall grasses, deep dark fertile soil, summers hot, winters cold, cereal crops grown, cattle and sheep graze

The Tropical Forest: orchids, green foliage all year, richest in plants and animals, undiscovered plants, swimming snakes and lizards, alligators

146. Life Science Vocabulary Vowelless Puzzle

147. Life Science's Odd One Out

1. jeans
2. chores
3. halitosis
4. prose
5. piano
6. carburetors
7. slouch
8. race
9. procurement
10. Big Ben
11. extraction
12. kangaroo
13. cheater
14. black mamba
15. sloth
16. exposure
17. hunting
18. diversification
19. eating
20. tail gunner
21. photosphere
22. plywood
23. yardstick
24. supercharger
25. horse

148. Plant World Tripod Connections

Answers will vary. These are suggestions.

1. reproduction
2. plant growth (time frames)
3. photosynthesis
4. tree growth
5. plant reproduction
6. trees
7. vegetables
8. reproduction
9. carbohydrates
10. plant structures
11. plant responses
12. legumes
13. plant requirements
14. osmosis

149. Adaptation of Colorization and Shape

1. unique
2. protecting
3. disguising
4. coloration
5. environment
6. difficult
7. black
8. doesn't
9. white
10. all
11. natural
12. easily
13. snow
14. shaped
15. similar
16. wings
17. resemblance
18. mimicry
19. poisonous
20. monarch

150. Life Science Search from Clues

1. chromosomes
2. cell division
3. addiction
4. hormones
5. marrow
6. propagation
7. spore formation
8. asexual reproduction
9. genes
10. carrier
11. natural selection
12. genetics
13. fossil
14. adaptation
15. ecosystem
16. food chain
17. embryo
18. pollination
19. endocrine glands
20. cerebrum
21. involuntary muscles
22. voluntary muscles
23. ligaments
24. carnivore
25. heredity

151. How One Life Form Is Like Another: Part One

Answers will vary. These are suggestions.

1. A shark is like a whale because both swim in the ocean.
2. A panda bear is like a grizzly bear because both can dwell in a forest environment.
3. A tiger is like a house cat because both are a form of feline or a member of the cat family.
4. A flamingo is like a sparrow because both are birds.
5. A rattlesnake is like a worm because both can be long and slender and both are limbless.
6. A tarantula is like a scorpion because the bite of the former and the sting of the latter can be very harmful to humans.
7. A housefly is like a dragonfly because both are insects.
8. A frog is like a toad because both are amphibians.

152. How One Life Form Is Like Another: Part Two

Answers will vary. These are suggestions.

1. Ancient dinosaurs are like the American alligator of today because both are or were reptiles.
2. A chicken is like a turkey because both are farmyard fowl.
3. An elk is like a deer because both can exist on a similar plant diet in the taiga or deciduous forest biome.
4. A horse is like a donkey because both can be ridden and carry burdens.
5. A bat is like a bird because both can fly.
6. A chimpanzee is like a gorilla because both are a form of ape.
7. A rat is like a squirrel because both are rodents that have two incisor teeth in each jaw adapted for gnawing.
8. A hare is like a kangaroo because both have rear legs adapted for propulsion.

153. How One Life Form Is <u>Not</u> Like Another: Part One

Answers will vary. These are suggestions.

1. The main difference between a rabbit and a hare is in the area of size. A hare is larger than a rabbit.

2. A porcupine differs from a skunk in the area of self-defense. A porcupine protects itself by a barbed quill system, whereas a skunk protects itself by means of a repugnant sprayable substance.

3. A dog is different from a wolf because a dog is more easily domesticated than a wolf.

4. An adult dolphin is usually smaller than an adult whale.

5. The head of an alligator is shorter and flatter than the head of a crocodile.

6. A kangaroo is much larger than a wallaby.

7. A cheetah can run faster than a leopard.

8. A tiger is a large stripped hunting cat, whereas a lion has no stripes.

9. A walrus is larger than a seal. A seal does not have two upper canine teeth forming tusks up to three feet long like a walrus does.

10. A hippopotamus is mainly a water dweller, whereas the rhinoceros is mainly a land dweller. The hippo does not have a snout horn, whereas the rhino may have one or two snout horns.

154. How One Life Form Is <u>Not</u> Like Another: Part Two

Answers will vary. These are suggestions.

1. A horse does not have stripes like a zebra.

2. A cow does not have a trunk or tusks like an elephant.

3. The Bactrian camel has two humps, while a dromedary has only one hump.

4. A buffalo is a form of plains-dwelling wild ox, whereas a deer is a more graceful mammal that is usually a woods dweller.

5. A butterfly has little knobs at the ends of its antenna, while a moth does not.

6. A turtle will dwell in the sea, whereas a tortoise lives only on land.

7. The dodo bird was a large non-flying bird that is now extinct, whereas the eagle is a large flying bird of prey whose population must be carefully monitored.

8. A lobster has a long narrow body with two big claws in front and eight legs, whereas a crab has a shorter, wide body with a tail folded under. The crab has four pairs of legs together with one pair of pincers.

9. A flea is a tiny, wingless insect that can jump. It lives as a parasite sucking the blood of animals, whereas a tick is an arachnid (spider) that can have a single pair of wings (dipterous).

10. An adult ostrich is larger than an adult emu.

155. A Resources Knowledge Puzzle

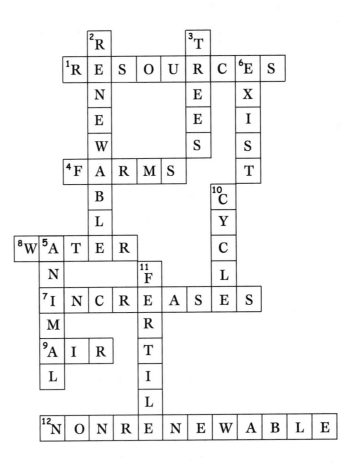

SECTION 8

156. How to Find Gold and Become Rich

1. winding
2. nuggets
3. correct
4. often
5. meander

6. river
7. tree
8. current
9. water
10. bend

11. bank
12. far
13. causes
14. slows
15. denses

157. A Hydrosphere Puzzle

1.	H	Y	D	R	O	S	P	H	E	R	E
2.	G	L	A	C	I	E	R				
3.	W	A	T	E	R	V	A	P	O	R	
4.	D	E	W								
5.	N	E	K	T	O	N					
6.	P	L	A	N	K	T	O	N			
7.	D	I	A	T	O	M	S				
8.	B	E	N	T	H	O	S				
9.	S	H	O	R	E	L	I	N	E		
10.	S	A	L	T							

158. All About Erosion

1. Erosion
2. rain
3. runoff
4. gradient
5. Plants

6. Porous
7. Avalanches
8. Creep
9. thawing
10. meandering

159. Double-Sided Erosion Synonyms

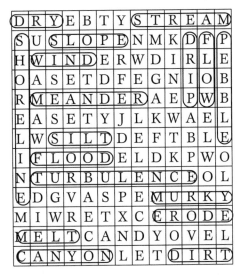

1. incline	10. melt
2. creek	11. turbulence
3. stone	12. overflow
4. arid	13. flow
5. gorge	14. drip
6. beach	15. decay
7. breeze	16. murky
8. dirt	17. curve
9. silt	

160. A Two-Space Water Puzzle

1. tasteless, colorless	6. expand, dense
2. oxygen, hydrogen	7. fresh, polar
3. electric, electrolysis	8. vegetables, 90%
4. solid, gas	9. 8,500, day
5. salt, oceans	10. removed, replenished

161. Liquid "Not the Same As" Vocabulary

Answers will vary. These are suggestions.

1. A solution is a homogenous combination wherein two or more substances do not retain their original identity, whereas a mixture is two or more substances that still retain their original identity while they are mixed together.

2. Ice is colder and harder than water.

3. A solute is a liquid solution that has had a solid, liquid, or gas dissolved in it, whereas a solvent is usually a liquid substance that can dissolve other materials or substances.

4. Homogenous in science usually refers to substances that are the same in quality and structure, whereas heterogenous in science refers to substances that are dissimilar or not the same in composition.

5. Water vapor contains a form of H_2O, whereas oxygen in the pure form contains only one substance, "oxygen."

6. An aquifer is a naturally occurring rock formation that contains water, whereas a reservoir can be a hand-built storage location for water.

7. Ocean water contains a large amount of salt, whereas Great Lakes water contains less salt than the ocean's and is considered to be "fresh water."

8. Diluted means for a substance to be thinned down or weakened by the addition of another substance (water), whereas concentrated means for a substance to increase in density or strength or power.

9. Saturated describes a substance that is completely filled to its capacity with another substance, whereas unsaturated describes a substance that is not filled or affected by another substance.

10. Solubility describes a substance that has the quality of dissolving or being dissolved, whereas permeability describes the ability of a substance to be passed through or soaked through by another substance.

162. Hydrology Vocabulary

1. glaciers
2. ground water
3. surface water
4. slough
5. aquifer
6. estuary
7. iceberg
8. Old Faithful geyser

163. Erosion: Eliminating the Negative and Explaining "Why"

Listed here are the circled answers. The explanations will vary.

1. tropical
2. oasis
3. talcum
4. capillaries
5. permanent
6. Aqueducts
7. estuary

164. Let's Tackle the Hydrosphere

1. RIVER, DELTA, SEDIMENT, WATER
2. MARINE, DIATOMS, PLANKTON, OCEANOGRAPHER
3. NEKTON, BENTHOS, COAST, REEF

Field Goal: the Abyssal Plain, or the Marianas Trench

165. A Water-Properties Spiral

D	S	⁴C	L	E	
N	X	I	S	A	
A	⁹E	■	T	R	
P	R	E	¹⁰M	⁵A	
X	I	S	E	D	
³E	⁸A	A	L	H	
N	S	H	T	E	
O	B	¹²P	I	R	
I	R	H	N	E	
S	O	G	G	⁶H	
N	S	I	¹¹H	E	¹F
E	B	⁷A	T	A	R
²T	S	E	Z	E	E

166. "Sea" the Ocean

1.	N	A	V	I	G	A	T	I	O	N
2.	E	U	S	T	A	S	Y			
3.	C	U	R	R	E	N	T	S		
4.	S	A	L	I	N	I	T	Y		
5.	G	U	Y	O	T					
6.	T	R	E	N	C	H				
7.	U	P	W	E	L	L	I	N	G	
8.	T	I	D	E						
9.	S	W	E	L	L					
10.	B	R	E	A	K	E	R			

167. Erosion Adjectives

Answers will vary.

168. The Erosion Wordsearch

G	S	L	A	N	D	S	L	I	D	E	K	R	C	F	R	S	A	T	T
R	T	A	T	H	W	Y	S	T	H	A	T	S	E	L	H	P	V	R	R
A	U	X	S	D	E	G	Y	S	E	T	Y	W	S	O	U	R	O	E	I
D	F	T	U	P	W	I	G	K	L	E	C	A	H	O	P	I	R	K	B
I	J	W	R	E	D	E	R	U	N	O	F	F	R	D	O	N	S	T	U
E	O	D	G	H	R	Y	P	O	L	K	E	R	E	P	L	G	E	R	T
N	S	O	M	E	A	N	D	E	R	E	R	I	L	L	K	S	H	J	A
T	T	V	O	L	I	G	J	L	E	R	I	L	J	A	O	B	E	R	R
N	O	R	U	M	N	L	G	E	Y	S	E	R	H	I	M	D	T	H	I
X	E	I	E	S	A	W	R	E	B	W	O	R	O	N	O	E	A	E	E
T	H	V	R	S	G	T	T	R	E	A	W	S	N	R	P	L	R	T	S
R	L	E	V	E	E	W	A	Q	U	I	F	E	R	S	E	T	X	A	S
S	C	R	R	I	C	T	H	E	J	X	O	T	S	I	T	A	E	T	H

1. runoff	8. gradient
2. landslide	9. drainage
3. meander	10. tributaries
4. levee	11. flood plain
5. aquifer	12. springs
6. geyser	13. delta
7. rill	14. river

SECTION 9

169. Weather Expressions with Missing Letters

1. wind sock
2. forecast
3. meteorology
4. thermometer
5. relative humidity
6. anemometer
7. barometer
8. wind vane

170. Grouping Climate Vocabulary

1. 4 per year, due to rotation and revolution
2. moisture, water vapor, saturation point
3. dry, hot, very little cloud cover
4. mercury, cold
5. cirrus, stratus, cumulus
6. cold heavy snow, blinding snowfall
7. spiral action, violent, destructive
8. affects wide area, has quieter eye, violent
9. seasonal wind, common in India
10. rain, snow, sleet, hail
11. lightning, thunder, cumulonimbus
12. water vapor, moisture, Pot o' Gold

171. Science/English Crossover Weather Grid

Answers may vary. These are suggestions.

	Nouns	Verbs	Adverbs	Adjectives
W	water	watered	westerly	wet
E	environment	expanding	ecologically	enormous
A	air	advanced	atmospherically	arid
T	tornado	thundered	torrentially	tropical
H	hail	heated	heavily	hot
E	energy	energize	easterly	erratic
R	rain	running	relatively	refreshing

172. How One Weather Item Is <u>Not</u> Like Another

Answers will vary. These are suggestions.

1. A tornado is a localized swirling storm, whereas a hurricane is a massive circular storm covering many square miles (kms).

2. Rain is a concentration of water droplets, whereas hail is frozen water that will hit the ground after intense upheaval of atmospheric conditions.

3. A cyclone is a large, irregularly occurring circular storm usually in the tropics, whereas a monsoon is a season of intense wind and rainfall that occurs every year in the area of southeast Asia and the Indian Ocean.

4. A blizzard is an intense winter snowstorm, whereas snow is the white, frozen form of winter precipitation.

5. A front is the leading edge of a weather change or the boundary between two air masses, whereas the jet stream is a high-level wind belt in the tropopause that blows from west to east.

6. A wind sock is the device that shows the direction of the wind. The wind speed is the miles or kilometers per hour the wind is actually traveling.

7. A downdraft is a downward current of air, wind, or gas, whereas an updraft is an upward current of air, wind, or gas in the atmosphere.

8. Lightning is the flash of light in the sky that results from the discharge of atmospheric electricity, whereas thunder is the sound that is made from the rapid expansion of atmospheric gases as lightning passes through that atmosphere.

9. An anemometer measures the force or speed of wind, whereas a barometer measures atmospheric pressure.

10. A forecast is the description of the weather in the future, whereas a weather broadcast is a media presentation of past, present, and future weather.

173. How One Weather Item Is Like Another

Answers will vary. These are suggestions.

1. Snow is rain in a frozen or solid form.

2. Sleet is like hail as both are a solid form of precipitation.

3. A wind is a strong breeze.

4. Summer heat is like winter cold because both are atmospheric conditions of the Earth relative to their seasons.

5. A wind sock and a wind vane can both indicate the direction of the wind.

6. Fog is a cloud close to the ground.

7. A hurricane is the name given to the same type of storm as a cyclone. The name hurricane is used in the northerly regions of the Earth, whereas the name cyclone is used in the tropics.

8. A thunderstorm is often called a cloudburst as both can be sudden downpours of precipitation.

174. Weather Speculation and Information

Answers will vary.

175. Design a Storm

Answers will vary.

176. Watch Out for Hail Damage

Wheat	$75.00	320	$24,000.00	$3.00	30	$28,800.00	90%	$25,920.00
Flax	$109.00	640	$69,760.00	$7.50	34	$163,200.00	92%	$150,144.00
Peas	$82.00	120	$9,840.00	$4.25	40	$20,400.00	64%	$13,056.00
Soybeans	$91.00	700	$63,700.00	$7.42	28	$145,432.00	99%	$143,977.68
Oats	$68.25	75	$5,118.75	$2.11	51	$8,070.75	68%	$5,488.11
Canola	$77.00	1,010	$77,770.00	$8.00	39	$315,120.00	100%	$315,120.00
Barley	$67.00	327	$21,909.00	$2.25	38	$27,958.50	64%	$17,893.44
Corn	$75.00	283	$21,225.00	$3.50	27	$26,743.50	98%	$26,208.63

177. Weather Vocabulary

SET A

1. Climate
2. Jet stream
3. Cyclone
4. Dewpoint
5. Monsoon
6. Precipitation
7. Blizzard
8. Exosphere
9. Evaporate
10. Hurricane
11. Atmosphere
12. Forecast
13. Tornado
14. Lightning

SET B

1. Turbulence
2. Isobar
3. Aeration
4. Westerlies
5. Anticyclone
6. Arid
7. Snow
8. Rain
9. Doldrums
10. Doppler
11. Environment
12. Evaporation
13. Freezing point
14. Ozone

178. Which Weather Pattern Is It?

1. hurricane
2. tornado
3. sleet
4. hail
5. rain
6. lightning
7. smog
8. snow

179. Weather Tripod Connections

1. storms
2. freezing
3. moisture
4. atmosphere
5. pollution
6. air
7. clouds
8. thunderstorm
9. tornado
10. forecasting
11. moisture
12. wind
13. temperature
14. wind

180. Climate/Weather Reverse Questions

Questions will vary. These are suggestions.

1. How does the air circulate above the Earth?
2. What are deserts?
3. What does the term "climate" actually refer to?
4. What does relative humidity tell us?
5. What does the term "dew point" refer to?
6. What are clouds?
7. What is fog?
8. How is a thunderstorm created?

181. Climate/Weather Expressions

1. doldrums
2. isothermal
3. temperate
4. desert
5. humidity
6. cyclonic
7. monsoons
8. Dust Bowl
9. fronts
10. greenhouse

182. It's Windy

1. quartz
2. deflation
3. Dust
4. abrasion
5. calm
6. windmills
7. dunes
8. breeze
9. gale
10. storm

183. Atmosphere: Eliminating the Negative and Explaining "Why"

Listed here are the circled answers. The explanations will vary.

1. compressed gases
2. uniformity
3. mercury thermometer
4. crust
5. jet propulsion
6. biosphere
7. liquid

184. What's the Weather Like Outside?

Answers will vary.

185. Facts About Tornadoes

A. 1. d   3. a   5. c
   2. f   4. b   6. e

B. 1. F   3. T   5. T   7. T
   2. T   4. T   6. T   8. F

186. Stormy Hurricane Clues

1. rotation
2. clockwise
3. eye
4. typhoon
5. pressure
6. land
7. Mexico
8. circular
9. Banguios
10. Willy-Willy

187. Weather Conditions

Answers will vary.

188. Atmosphere Expressions

1. Nitrogen
2. protect
3. Oxygen
4. volume
5. barometer
6. troposphere
7. jet stream
8. convection
9. wind
10. pollution
11. smog
12. temperature

189. The Solstice and Equinox

1. solstice
2. stops
3. time
4. most
5. southerly
6. each
7. path
8. farthest
9. longest
10. night
11. December
12. sun's
13. south
14. shortest
15. year
16. equal
17. length
18. equinox
19. autumnal
20. 12

190. The Weather Terms Wordsearch

U	P	D	R	A	F	T	H	U	N	D	E	R	S	T	O	R	M	S	T
B	E	R	M	Y	D	A	T	E	S	O	H	T	R	E	J	O	N	I	N
I	S	O	T	H	E	R	M	S	T	W	C	S	A	T	S	O	T	S	O
H	R	E	O	J	N	S	T	O	A	N	U	T	O	R	N	A	D	O	B
S	A	R	E	G	J	K	H	N	R	D	I	M	K	A	T	H	C	B	R
W	I	E	A	T	Y	M	A	G	E	R	N	I	U	P	W	E	R	A	N
A	R	B	A	V	C	A	I	E	V	A	W	T	S	O	R	N	K	R	A
S	M	R	H	J	L	I	L	R	L	F	O	R	E	C	A	S	T	S	D
T	A	N	P	L	E	R	A	O	F	T	G	R	W	Q	I	A	H	Y	F
O	S	D	E	W	A	B	S	W	E	Z	U	X	T	U	N	K	R	I	R
R	S	J	E	T	S	T	R	E	A	M	B	R	N	A	T	A	S	G	O
E	H	U	R	R	I	C	A	N	E	D	N	A	E	S	R	E	H	G	N
F	U	N	N	E	L	S	M	E	T	E	O	R	O	L	O	G	I	S	T

1. updraft
2. thunderstorm
3. jet stream
4. isotherms
5. tornado
6. forecasts
7. funnel
8. meteorologist
9. air mass
10. front
11. isobars
12. downdraft
13. hurricane
14. rain
15. hail